PUFFIN BOOKS
RABINDRANATH TAGORE

Monideepa Sahu is a former banker, who had a whale of a time writing her fantasy adventure novel, *Riddle of the Seventh Stone*. Her short stories for both adults and young people have been widely anthologized in India and abroad. She enjoys concocting tall tales, and can also wax eloquent on deathly serious subjects. She lives in Bangalore with her extended family of people, a vintage PC and countless arthropods. You can connect with her at www.monideepa.blogspot.in

Other books in the *Puffin Lives* series

RABINDRANATH TAGORE

THE RENAISSANCE MAN

MONIDEEPA SAHU

PUFFIN BOOKS

An imprint of Penguin Random House

PUFFIN BOOKS

USA | Canada | UK | Ireland | Australia
New Zealand | India | South Africa | China | Singapore

Puffin Books is part of the Penguin Random House group of companies
whose addresses can be found at global.penguinrandomhouse.com

Published by Penguin Random House India Pvt. Ltd
4th Floor, Capital Tower 1, MG Road,
Gurugram 122 002, Haryana, India

Penguin
Random House
India

First published in Puffin by Penguin Books India 2013

Text copyright © Monideepa Sahu 2013

All rights reserved

10 9 8 7 6 5 4 3 2

ISBN 9780143332299

Typeset in Bembo by Eleven Arts, Delhi
Printed at Manipal Technologies Limited, India

www.penguin.co.in

MIX
Paper | Supporting
responsible forestry
FSC® C043100

This is a legitimate digitally printed version of the book and therefore might not
have certain extra finishing on the cover.

Contents

Acknowledgements

I would like to thank Prof. Mohammad A. Quayum, Professor of English at the International Islamic University Malaysia (IIUM); Adjunct Professor in the School of Humanities, Flinders University, Australia; author, editor and translator of Tagore, for his helpful advice.

I would also thank Dr Sandipan Sen, Associate Professor of English at Ananda Mohan College, Kolkata, and Tanushree Gangopadhyay, journalist, for their guidance and encouragement.

Thanks are due to Sudeshna Shome Ghosh, Sohini Mitra and Mimi Basu, the editors who worked tirelessly behind the scenes to make this book happen.

Thanks also to my supportive writer friends from various on and offline groups, and to Baba and Siddhartha for their advice, encouragement and for bearing with me.

1 ✒ It All Began in the Thakurbari

One hundred and fifty years ago when the British Raj was at the peak of its glory, Calcutta flourished as an important hub of commerce and culture. In this big city, a boy named Rabi lived in a sprawling mansion with his brothers, sisters, aunts, uncles and cousins. He was the fourteenth among fifteen brothers and sisters. However the last child died young, so Rabi grew up as the youngest in the family.

In those days, Calcutta was quite different from how it is today. There were no trams, buses or cars. People travelled in horse-drawn carts, and those who could afford it rode palanquins. Life was slow and relaxed. While Rabi was very young, gaslights and electricity hadn't yet been introduced into the city. The children studied their evening lessons by the light of oil lamps. When kerosene lanterns were first brought into Thakurbari, the family mansion of the Tagores where Rabi lived, everyone was amazed by the bright light.

One day Rabi was excited to hear of a fairy-tale place in his home. It was the king's house. A cousin of Rabi's age described it as a wonderland filled with enchanting games and toys. Yes, it really was here, in this very house, Rabi's playmate would assert. Why, she had

1

just been there this very morning. Rabi looked into every room and corridor, but he never could find out who the king was, nor discover his enchanted kingdom.

Rabi's father Maharshi Debendranath Tagore's private room was another magical place. The Maharshi was often away from home, and the room would be locked up. Rabi would secretly steal into this mysterious room, smelling of deep secrets. He would curl up on the sofa, look out at the empty terrace lit by the blazing midday sun and lose himself in daydreams. He was fascinated by a certain delightful object in the Maharshi's room. It was a water tap! This wonderful machine, which had just been introduced to the people of Calcutta, carried water all the way up to the third floor and into the Maharshi's bathroom. Rabi would sneak in at the oddest hours and turn on the shower. He was thrilled to enjoy this forbidden pleasure.

The Tagore family was among the richest and most prominent of those times. However, little Rabi and the other children of the house led a spartan life without the slightest hint of luxury. Rabi did not remember wearing socks before he was ten. As for warm wraps, one plain shirt on top of another was considered enough to keep out the winter chill. The children did own slippers, but usually kept them as far as possible from their feet. It never occurred to Rabi to curse his luck for the missing socks and woollies. But he was unhappy because the family tailor didn't stitch pockets into his shirts. After all, even the poorest children had precious little treasures to store in their pockets.

Servants employed to care for the Tagore children kept a strict watch over them all. Rabi and the other little ones spent much of their time in the servants' quarters. The grand lifestyle, clothes, feasts, entertainment and intellectual discussions of the elders seemed far away from Rabi's world. In the 19th century, Bengal was swept by radical social, cultural and religious transformations. Historians call this the Bengal Renaissance. The Tagore family was at the forefront of these changes, leading the way in literature, arts and culture, social and religious reform. Little Rabi could, however, catch only glimpses of this charmed circle of his elders. Their world was as yet out of bounds for a child like him.

Rabi learned to make the most of everything because privileges did not come to him easily. The children weren't allowed to leave the mansion. Rabi however tried to catch glimpses of the world outside like a bird from a cage. He found joy in his surroundings by colouring everything with his imagination. It was fun for him to explore the huge house and peep out from the terrace at the street below. Hawkers would come and go, calling out their wares. On the other side of their boundary wall, Rabi could see a calm pond with a banyan tree on its bank. He would observe his neighbours coming one by one for a dip. By noon, when all the bathers had left, the swans and ducks would remain, diving into the water for snails or preening themselves with their beaks.

This dreamy boy loved stories and books. His introduction to literature began with the books popular among the household servants. A Bengali translation of Chanakya's shlokas and Krittibas' Ramayana were their favourites.

One of the family retainers employed to look after the Tagore children was Ishwar, a former village schoolmaster. Ishwar was a grave man, who spoke in high-flown language. To keep the children busy in the evenings, he would recite from the Bengali translations of the Ramayana by Krittibas and the Mahabharata, and engage in discussions around the ancient epics. Rabindranath was enchanted by the beautiful rhythms of Krittibas' poetry.

Rabi's elder brother Somendranath and his sister's son Satyabrata (Satya), both two years his senior, were his constant companions. When a tutor was called to teach them their letters, Rabi joined the group. The words and the rhythm of Bengali nursery rhymes filled little Rabi's soul with wonder. This was his first initiation to the magic of poetry. Long after the words were spoken, their rhythm and musicality lingered on in his mind.

★★★★

One cloudy day, Rabi was playing on the long verandah at the entrance of the mansion. 'Policeman! Policeman!' Satya cried as he ran in frantically. Rabi had only vague notions about the grim duties of policemen. If someone pointed out a wrongdoer, the policeman would catch him and the man would disappear forever. A policeman was like a crocodile, which dives into the deep river with its hapless prey. Where could the little boy hide from the terrors awaiting him in the police station? Rabi rushed into his mother's room for protection. But she didn't seem particularly upset. Despite her calm reaction, Rabi didn't feel it safe to leave her side. To soothe his mind, he took up a well-worn copy of the Ramayana which belonged to his grandmother, and began to read. He soon forgot the terrors of the police. Tears welled up in his eyes as he sat on the doorstep caught up in the narative.

As Rabi grew, his heart filled with wonder at the beauty of this earth. The soil, the trees, the water, the sky would all speak to him in those dreamy days of childhood, never giving him the chance to harbour a sad thought. He often wondered at the fact that only the outermost layer of the earth could be seen. What lay underneath? When wooden pillars were planted into the ground to erect tents for the winter festival in his home, Rabi would watch with bated breath. The pits were dug deeper and deeper, until the digger seemed to disappear into it. But still, Rabi could not discover the secret route through which fairy-tale princes entered 'Patal Puri'. If only they would dig a little deeper, he thought, the mystery might finally be solved.

The mystery of the blue dome of the sky was equally exciting. One day, their tutor told them that the blue sky was not a solid barrier at all. 'You can build as many stairs as you like and go on climbing. Nothing will stand in your way,' he said.

'What if you added more, and more, and even more steps?' asked Rabi. He was amazed to learn that even an endless number of stairs would make no difference. The schoolmasters of this world must have been extraordinary people to understand such mind-boggling ideas.

Rabi grew up in a huge household, where people were always doing new and unusual things. The Tagore elders once held a planchette to summon spirits of dead people. The pencil moved to spell out the name of Kailash Mukherjee. He had served the family for many years as a secretary before his death. 'Tell us what happens after death,' everyone asked the spirit. Pat came the reply: 'You want to cheat and find out what I've learnt only after dying? Sorry. I won't tell.'

★★★★

One day Rabi watched his brother and Satya going off to school. He felt insignificant and unworthy when they left him behind. Until then, Rabi had never sat in a carriage or gone outside the house. So when Satya described his daily travels to school in glowing detail, Rabi could stand it no more. The only way he could prove his fitness for school was to scream at the top of his lungs.

'Just you wait!' said his tutor, thrashing him soundly to drive out all foolish notions. 'One day you will cry much more to be excused from school.' Rabi would never hear a more accurate prophecy in his life.

The power of his tears pushed Rabi into his first school at a tender age. In later years, he could hardly remember what education he had received there. But the frequent punishments remained etched forever in his memory. Rabi soon framed a strategy to overcome the humiliation of being a lowly schoolboy. In a special corner of the balcony at home, he started his very own class. The railings were his students. Holding a wooden cane in his hand, Rabi played the tough schoolmaster. It was strictly determined from the very beginning, which railings were good students, and which were duffers. The naughty and dull railings got beaten so much, that if had they been alive, they would gladly have sacrificed their lives to get some peace. When he grew up, Rabi understood the huge difference between rows of railings and rows of students. Many years later, he launched his own experiments to make learning more interesting for young people.

One of Rabi's schoolmasters was particularly foul-tempered. Rabi would sit silently in his class, dreaming of solving all the complicated problems of this world. He seriously considered how to win battles without the help of weapons. First, ferocious animals like tigers would have to be properly trained. Then rows of them should be placed at the forefront of the battlefield. This would set the stage for a grand battle, and then it would be easy to gain victory with the use of one's physical prowess.

Every morning before lessons, the boys would gather in the school's gallery and recite a poem in a sing-song voice. This was probably an attempt by the authorities to make learning fun. But young Rabi, like most of the other little boys, could not understand the English words. The children mispronounced the difficult foreign words as gibberish—'Colloki, puloki singil melaling melaling

melaling.' Many years later, Rabindranath figured out some of the words with great effort. The line probably meant 'Full of glee, singing merrily, merrily, merrily.' However, the meaning of the first word, 'colloki', would remain an eternal mystery.

As Rabi grew older, tutors were retained to teach the three boys subjects beyond the regular school course. The routine started at dawn with wrestling lessons from a champion. Lessons in physics, literature, geometry, algebra, history and geography followed. As soon as the three boys returned from school, the drawing and gymnastics instructors took charge. The boys would finally get a break after nine p.m., when the English lessons ended. Even Sundays brought no respite. That's when a master came to give them singing lessons.

Their tutor Aghor Babu was a student of the Medical College. His rock-solid health and unfailing devotion to duty disappointed Rabi and his companions. One evening, it was raining cats and dogs. Knee-deep water flooded the streets. The clock ticked on. The unthinkable had happened. Aghor Babu was five minutes late! Hearts thumping, prayers on their lips, the boys scanned the street below hoping for a reprieve from the day's lessons. Oh no! The familiar black umbrella appeared, invincible against the deluge. Aghor Babu actually had the courage to turn up in their lane braving the flood.

Aghor Babu always tried his best to make lessons as interesting as possible. One day he displayed before the boys the bones of a human voice box. As he explained its intricate functions, disappointment overwhelmed Rabi. He had imagined that the entire human being, and not a small mechanical part of the body, performed the miracle of speech.

★★★★

Young Rabi often felt shackled by the narrow restrictions of the school routine. At home, his tutors instructed him on much beyond the school syllabus. He was taught scientific facts and theories in Bengali, but he was not encouraged to discover connections to the wider world beyond the pages of dull textbooks. Tutors made him dissect beautiful poetry according to the dry rules of grammar. It ruined Rabi's enjoyment and made learning painful. He studied hard but felt that he learnt little. Rabi would have preferred to spend time idling as he pleased. He could then allow his imagination to fly free. But time spent forcibly doing something dull and pointless was a dead waste he later felt when he grew up.

Relief came unexpectedly. One day Satya needed to borrow a book from his grandfather, Maharshi Debendranath Tagore. Eager to impress his learned elder, Satya made a formal speech, framing his request in stilted high-flown Bengali. No scholar could have found fault with his words, but the Maharshi sensed that the boys were learning Bengali that was too stylized. He feared that they would soon lose touch with the true language of the people. He called Rabi, Somendranath and Satya upstairs to his room and announced, 'No more Bengali lessons from now on.' The three boys wanted to dance and celebrate.

Many years later, the grown-up Rabindranath sensed the benefits of primary education in one's mother tongue. He felt that when children were forced to learn through an alien language, they wasted much energy trying to make sense of it. This pointless effort killed their natural curiosity and spirit. Rabindranath realized that his elders had taken a bold step in teaching their children their mother tongue, Bengali, in an era when English education was prized and preferred by India's elite.

Soon the boys were transferred to Bengal Academy, a school run by Anglo-Indians. The boys felt proud and grown-up, a step closer to freedom. Rabi was relieved to find that his classmates were simply naughty, but not mean. Their pranks were not meant to offend. The three boys, however, couldn't understand a word of what was being taught. So they made no efforts to study. The school authorities were pleased that the Tagore family paid their fees punctually. Hence nobody took any notice of whether the Tagore boys learnt their lessons. The best thing about this school was that high expectations were not thrust upon the children. Learning Latin did not become unbearable. Punishments were not handed out for minor errors.

Though the usual tortures were kept at bay, the academy was still a typical educational institution. Rabi found the classrooms cold and forbidding. The walls were like sentries guarding imprisoned children. The place was like a big box with compartments. It contained no colours, no pictures, no decorations; nothing to make the place attractive for children. Rabi wondered whether the notion of making learning appealing, had ever even been considered in this place. Every morning when he stepped into the school's cramped courtyard, he felt like running away.

One day, Rabi would establish his own school where students would be free to make mistakes and learn from them. All the little sins from his own childhood and his boyish miseries would still return to haunt the grown-up Rabindranath, whenever one of the teachers became angry and intolerant. He firmly believed that children should not be harshly judged by adults. He would advocate every child's birthright to run free, like a pure, clear stream.

The Thakurbari (literally translated as Tagore House) in Jorasanko, northern Kolkata, was built in the 18th century. Rabindranath was born here in 1861. The mansion continues to stand in Dwarkanath Tagore Lane in Kolkata, a stone's throw from Shovabazar Metro Station on Rabindra Sarani. The brick-red painted building and expansive gardens have now been restored. Rabindranath's rooms have been arranged to appear the way they would have been in his time. Visitors today can see the room where Rabindranath was born, his wife Mrinalini Devi's kitchen and the bed on which the Nobel laureate drew his last breath. Thakurbari today houses the Tagore family museum. There are photographs taken in those times, and also paintings by Rabindranath.

The Rabindra Bharati University initially began functioning here in 1961 to mark the birth centenary of the poet. The university focuses upon higher education in the humanities and in the performing and fine arts. If you happen to be in Kolkata, the Thakurbari is well worth a visit. Within walking distance are the well-known mansions of other rich and famous Bengalis of Rabindranath's time, such as the Marble Palace and the Shovabazar Rajbari.

2 ✒ The Budding Poet

As Rabi progressed in school, the struggle with lessons intensified at home. After school, Rabi wanted to play, watch the world go by from his window or simply curl up with a book. But that's when tutors came to Thakurbari to train him to tackle the tricks and twists of learning English. The textbooks then weren't illustrated and appealing to children, as they are now. Dark, thick covers and difficult language made their subject even less appealing. Rows of words for spelling lessons, broken up into syllables, seemed to point their accent marks like bayonets at young Rabi.

Some of his dedicated tutors though, provided a silver lining. Sundays weren't Sundays without Shri Sitanath Dutt's lessons on natural sciences. One day, he demonstrated how heated water would become lighter and rise from the bottom of the vessel. Rabi was thrilled to learn that water was an independent component of milk. When milk was heated, water would escape as steam, resulting in thicker milk.

Meanwhile, Rabi's considerably older nephew Jyotiprakash had already begun reading English literature. He would recite Hamlet's soliloquies with enthusiasm. One afternoon, Jyotiprakash summoned

Rabindranath to his room and announced, 'You must write poems.' He then proceeded to explain the basic rules of rhyming and prosody. Until then, Rabi had come across poems only in print. He thought they were perfectly polished products created with no revisions or changes.

Rabi was barely seven or eight years old at that time. Could he really compose a poem all by himself? Taking up some words, he strung them together into rhyme. His heart danced at the prospect of writing. He managed to get a notebook with blue pages and drew uneven lines on them with a pencil. And then he let himself go, composing rhymes in a big, childish scrawl.

One of his older brothers was especially proud of Rabi's poetic skills, and would turn the whole household topsy-turvy to gather an audience for the young poet's recitals. One day the two brothers were emerging from the ground floor reception area of Thakurbari, having proclaimed Rabi's poetic skills to the subjects and employees of their estates. They then spotted the editor of *National Paper*, Shri Nabagopal Mitra, and cornered him. Rabi wasted no time and read out his latest composition, standing right there in the courtyard. At the end of the recitation, the editor smiled and praised the poem. He suggested that Rabi replace some unusual words with simpler ones. But Rabi had pinned his aspirations on the complicated and unusual word usage. Now the editor of *National Paper* had actually laughed over it. Rabi couldn't help but feel that this great editor was incapable of appreciating true poetry. He responded to Nabagopal Mitra's criticism by leaving his poem unchanged.

Rabi's first blue notebook filled up with words of all shapes and sizes, running in uneven lines like rows of insects. The pages soon turned dog-eared in the boy's grubby hands. With time, the notebook became tattered and was lost to oblivion.

In those times it was rare for young boys, or even grown-ups, to write poetry. One day Gobinda Babu, the school superintendent, summoned Rabi to his office. The stout, dark gentleman inspired fear and awe among the schoolboys. Rabi entered Gobinda Babu's chamber with a thumping heart, dreading the worst.

'So you write poems?' Gobinda Babu asked.

Rabi didn't hesitate to confess that he did. Gobinda Babu then directed him to write a poem on some noble moral theme. Rabi was pleasantly surprised to be assigned such a happy task. He dashed off some lines and produced them the very next day. Gobinda Babu made him stand in front of his class and recite the poem. The instructive effect of Rabi's moral poem wasn't encouraging at all. Rabi's classmates certainly did not like the young poet because of his prominence. 'Rabi couldn't have written the poem by himself,' the boys whispered audibly among themselves.

'I can show you the book from which he has copied it,' said one boy. Of course the others never asked to see the book. They needed to believe, and producing proofs may have spoiled what they had already convinced themselves about. Soon, many pretenders emerged from the class to claim the name and fame of being a poet.

★★★★

Rabi's father Maharshi Debendranath Tagore used to travel frequently on long journeys. As a boy, Rabi had to satisfy his curiosity with brief glimpses of this fascinating stranger when he made sudden, brief visits home. Rabi had to remain with the other young ones of the family in the servants' area, and couldn't quite manage to approach his father. When the Maharshi came home, the entire household would be abuzz. The elders would wear good clothes and tidy themselves up, taking care to spit out the *paan* from their mouths before approaching him. Rabi's mother Sarada Devi would spend hours in the kitchen supervising the meals. The children were warned not to prance about or make too much noise, so that the Maharshi would not be disturbed.

Debendranath Tagore was a learned and deeply pious man, who knew Sanskrit, Persian and English, as well as his native Bengali. Educated in the traditions of Western philosophy as well as in Hindu scriptures, he had a deep knowledge of our spiritual heritage. He wrote several works in Bengali. One of his books, *Vedantic Doctrines Vindicated* (1845), was translated into English. His *Brahmo-Dharma* (The Religion of God) a commentary in Bengali on the Sanskrit scriptures, is considered to be a masterpiece.

Taking the lead in religious and social reform movements of his time, the Maharshi was among the first to embrace the reformist Brahmo religion. During one of his visits home, he arranged the sacred thread ceremony for his three youngest sons, who were between ten to twelve years of age. The boys were made in advance to practice the appropriate mantras from the Upanishads, which were compiled in Brahmo religious texts. The Maharshi referred to the appropriate Vedic mantras and tried his best to follow the ancient Vedic rituals for the ceremony. With their heads shaved and dressed in austere garments, Rabi and his two brothers were confined to a room in the Thakurbari for three whole days. They didn't quite spend the days in strict discipline. In fact, they had great fun tugging at each other's earrings and thumping and jumping to distract the servants downstairs.

As a newly-ordained Brahmin, Rabi tried his best to recite the Gayatri Mantra properly. He didn't understand the deeper significance of the chant at the tender age of eleven. What mattered most was not that he understood the complete literal meaning, but that the mantra, with its beauty and rhythm, resonated in his soul.

After his head was tonsured during his sacred thread ceremony, Rabi dreaded returning to school. Even if his English classmates didn't toss any objects at his shaven head, they would surely shower him with ridicule. The Maharshi's invitation to join him for a journey to the Himalayas came at this opportune time. Rabi wanted to shout out his joy till his voice reached the clouds.

On the big day before setting out, the Maharshi assembled everyone in the household and conducted prayers. After touching the feet of all the elders, Rabindranath followed his father into the carriage. The Maharshi had specially ordered a smart outfit for his son, with detailed instructions on the quality and colour of the cloth. Rabi was wearing such fine clothes for the first time in his life. He even had an embroidered velvet cap. Rabi did not want to cover his shaven head. But the Maharshi noticed every time his son took the cap off, and told him to put it back on again.

The Maharshi was a clear thinker, who carefully planned even the smallest projects. He never settled for shoddy work, and everyone took care in following his instructions. Small compromises may not have done any material harm, but Rabi felt that it hurt the Maharshi's strong sense of order and discipline.

Leaving the city for the first time in his life, Rabi was thrilled to ride in trains through the green countryside. Everything was so new: the fields, villages, and big cities like Allahabad and Kanpur. Rabi's father took him to the Golden Temple in Amritsar and they listened to chanting from Sikh holy scriptures. Finally they reached the snow-capped mountains of Dalhousie. During their stay there, Rabi would sing religious songs to his father. Such activities helped shape his strong spiritual base.

Rabi thoroughly enjoyed those first travel experiences. Each detail seemed so unique and precious. As a grown-up, Rabindranath would in later years pretend to be a visitor from abroad while passing through the streets of Kolkata. He realized that there is plenty to marvel at even in one's familiar city. One only had to be curious, attentive and appreciate one's surroundings. In later years, Rabindranath travelled all over India and the world, involving himself in the sights and sounds, the people and their customs, with deep interest. In this way, he imbibed many ideas and influences.

The Maharshi, while being intensely disciplined, could also be relaxed and fun. He allowed Rabi to freely explore on his own. He treated his young son with gentle humour, taking his childish suggestions seriously. During these travels, the Maharshi would also take time out to teach lessons from books. But when Rabi felt sleepy or exhausted, the Maharshi would excuse him. He also handed Rabi some money and the charge to wind his expensive gold watch daily. This, the Maharshi felt, would teach the boy practical responsibilities. The watch, however, suffered from overenthusiastic winding, and soon had to be sent to Calcutta for repairs. With his father's encouragement, Rabi also offered alms to beggars they came across on the way. At the end of the day the accounts often ran short. One day however, Rabi found extra money after checking the accounts.

'I'll have to appoint you as my cashier,' said the Maharshi with a smile. 'My money has grown in your hands.'

Meanwhile, Rabi continued to write new poems. Feeling quite grown-up at the ripe age of eleven, he aspired to be counted among the ranks of poets one day.

A new hardbound diary had replaced that first tattered blue notebook. Sitting in the open under a coconut tree and filling the pages with grand words seemed the most poetic thing to do. He composed a heroic epic on Prithviraj, containing eloquent descriptions of bravery. However, the epic too vanished somewhere, along with the diary. Following the old blue notebook into oblivion, it left no trace or forwarding address.

Once, while Maharshi Debendranath Tagore was on a journey to the Himalayas, there were rumours in Calcutta of an impending attack by the Russians. An elderly aunt, with the best intentions, related this news with imaginative flourish to Rabi's mother. 'A revolution is coming. The Russians could swoop upon us like a terrible comet anytime!' Sarada Devi was naturally upset, and turned to the family for help. The elders didn't pay much attention to what they felt was needless anxiety. Sarada Devi finally approached Rabi in desperation.

'Write a letter to your father and warn him about the Russian attack,' she said.

Rabi hadn't yet learnt to write letters properly. He took the help of Mahananda Munshi, and the letter was written at last in the dry style of a zamindar's clerk. A reply soon arrived from the Maharshi:

'Don't be afraid. I'll chase away all the Russians myself.'

Even such strong assurances did not to ease Sarada Devi's fear of the Russians. But Rabi's respect and awe of his father rose even higher. From then on, he pestered the munshi every day to help him write to the Maharshi. The munshi was forced by the eager boy to draft several letters. Rabi thought that handing over correspondence to the munshi was enough. Little did he know that his letters were never sent to the Himalayas at all.

3 Rabi's Family

Rabi returned home to a hero's welcome. Until then, he had been an insignificant little boy, barely noticed because he had always been a part of the familiar surroundings. After his travels to far-off lands, everyone began to take notice of him. The attention began during the return journey home. English gentlemen and ladies on the train took great interest in the handsome boy travelling with only a single attendant. The Maharshi was continuing his journey around the hills, and would return home much later.

The trip to the Himalayas marked the end of the servants' rule over Rabi. The doors to the *antahpur* or private family area ruled over by the ladies, were now thrown open to him. His mother Sarada Devi welcomed him to take pride of place in the gatherings held in her private chambers. Everyone wanted Rabi, the little traveller, to talk about his adventures.

Sarada Devi was thrilled to hear that during his travels, Rabi had read the original Sanskrit Ramayana by Valmiki, with the help of his father. Most adults managed to read only the Bengali version by Krittibas. So this was a great feat for her eleven-year-old son.

'Please recite and explain some shlokas from that Ramayana to us, dear,' she once said.

Rabi had read only a portion of the epic from a simple primer for beginners. When he tried to read it again, he realized that he had forgotten most of it. But his mother was eagerly waiting for a demonstration of her son's remarkable learning. How could Rabi disappoint her? So he read aloud some sections from the book. However there was much difference between what Valmiki had composed, and Rabi's commentary.

Believing that her child had achieved the impossible, Sarada Devi wanted to impress everyone. 'You must recite this before Dwijendra,' she insisted and, ignoring Rabi's protests, summoned her learned eldest son. Rabi had no choice. His bluff would be called. Humiliation was inevitable. Thankfully, Dwijendranath must have been preoccupied at that moment with some new composition of his own. He heard Rabi's recitation of a couple of Sanskrit shlokas, but showed no interest in listening to their Bengali explanation. 'Very nice,' he mumbled absent-mindedly, and carried on with his own pursuits.

As a child, Rabi could not freely mingle as much as he wished with the ladies of the family. He had always yearned to be a part of the mysterious world of the women's quarters of the mansion, imagining it as a place where there was no school, and no strict masters. Nobody had to give detailed accounts of their studies and movements there and everyone was free to do as they pleased.

Rabi's sister Barnakumari took lessons along with him and the other children from the same Neelkamal Master. However, there was no pressure upon her to study. Every morning, Rabi and the other boys rushed to get ready for school. Rabi would wistfully watch Barnakumari saunter about inside the house, swinging her long braids as though she didn't have a care in the world.

When a new, bejewelled bride entered the Thakurbari, the mystery of the women's quarters deepened. The new bride came from elsewhere, but she now belonged in the family. She was at once a stranger, and also one of their own. Rabindranath wanted to make friends with her. He wanted to enter the women's chambers, examine the beautiful curios in the glass showcases and take part in their activities. But if Rabi managed to go near, Barnakumari always chased him away, making him feel sad and unwelcome. But things changed after his return from the Himalayas. Rabi was now given a warm welcome into the *antahpur*.

The women of Thakurbari were remarkable. They were among the first women of Bengal to emerge from the purdah, receive the benefits of education and participate in social reform movements such as widow remarriage. They were accomplished achievers and trailblazers in their own right. They played as vital a role as the Tagore men in creating a literary and artistic environment within the household, which nurtured Rabindranath as a budding poet. In an age when women rarely ventured out of the home, ladies from the Tagore family set examples of courage and initiative. In the 19th century, an era when respectable Indian ladies were bound by strong social restrictions of their houses, Rabindranath's eldest sister-in-law Jnanadanandini sailed alone to England. Sushama Tagore was a fierce advocate of women's empowerment. Chandramukhi and Kadambini were the first two female graduates of India while Protiva Tagore opened up the realms of music and theatre to women by preparing musical notations for Brahmo sangeet and Hindustani classical music.

When Rabindranath was young, most upper-class women were secluded by the purdah. Rabindranath's mother Sarada Devi, was a traditional Hindu lady who spent her entire life in purdah. In her time, women from respectable families of Bengal were not permitted to ride in carriages or wear shoes. When Sarada Devi wished to take a dip in the holy Ganga, she was carried there in a palanquin. The bearers dipped the entire palanquin into the river, while she continued to sit inside, hidden from the world. Yet Sarada Devi too, was progressive for her time. She supported the artistic environment of Thakurbari and appreciated the poetry written by Rabindranath as a child. Sarada Devi died when Rabindranath was still young. The other women of the family immediately took him under their protective wings. They never gave Rabi a chance to realize, at that tender age, the terrible nature of his loss.

Being a reformist family, the Tagores supported the education of women. As a pillar of the progressive religious movement, the Brahmo Samaj, the Maharshi educated his own daughters to set an example for society. Together with his close friend and fellow reformer Keshub Chandra Sen, he made significant contribution in spreading education in his country, and bringing it within the reach of everyone. The Maharshi also spoke strongly against sati, the practice of burning widows on the funeral pyres of their husbands.

The Maharshi arranged for home tutors and also gave the girls regular lessons in science himself. He took the lead in admitting his eldest daughter Saudamini to the newly opened Bethune School for girls. One day, seeing the unusual sight of a beautiful and fair-skinned little girl travelling to school in a palanquin, a policeman stopped them, suspecting she was a kidnapped British child.

Rabindranath's elder sister Swarnakumari Devi Ghoshal's outstanding literary and intellectual achievements stood out even among the Tagore women. Educated by home tutors, she was married very young, and became the mother of four children by nineteen. Yet she published her first work, a historical novel about Prithviraj Chauhan, when she was just fifteen. She continued to write for the next fifty years; stories, poems, dramas and novels, as well as works for children. She also edited literary journals, organized women's groups, engaged in social work and actively participated in nationalist activities.

As he grew up, Rabindranath would bounce off ideas on poetry, music and drama with many of the ladies in his family, particularly his sister-in-law Kadambari

Devi, and later with his wife Mrinalini Devi. Others, like his eldest daughter Bela, inspired characters in his stories. Bela, according to Rabindranath, was just like Mini, the adorable little Bengali girl who struck up an unlikely friendship with an Afghan fruit seller in 'Kabuliwalla'. Mini's dialogues in the story were almost entirely taken from Bela's in real life.

Inspired by all these marvellous women in his family, Rabindranath filled his novels and short stories with unforgettable women characters, portraying them with depth and sensitivity. Strong and confident women such as Charu in *Nashtanir*, Bimala in *Gharey Bairey*, Mrinmayee, Chandara, Ela, Anandamoyee and many more have a prominent position in the world of Rabindranath's fiction. Noteworthy among the other fiery and memorable women created by Rabindranath are Damini of *Chaturanga*, the woman who revolts against male-dominated social rules; Giribala of *Manbhanjan*, who deserts her husband and beats him at his own game; Mrinal of *Stree-r Patro*, who writes a letter to her spouse explaining in detail her choice to leave him: and Binodini, the beautiful and highly accomplished young widow protagonist of *Chokher Bali*, who continues to fascinate readers with her darkly enticing personality as she asks hard-hitting questions and challenges her unjust fate. Lively, confident and clear-thinking, these women are a far cry from the traditional image of women as timid, long-suffering victims. These protagonists portray Rabindranath's concerns about the condition of women and the need for their advancement. His stories show his faith in progress and in freeing women from oppressive customs while preserving age-old positive values.

While Rabindranath admired the 19th century Western concept of liberalism, he was not quite a radical revolutionary. He supported social change and advancement, but felt it should come about by changing people's hearts, rather than by imposing new ideas upon them. He tried to bring about this change through his poems and stories, by expressing his ideals in a memorable way. He complied with society in his personal life, but expressed his liberal ideas in his writings.

Notun Bouthan and Jyoti Dada

Kadambari Devi, the lively young wife of Rabindranath's elder brother Jyotirindranath, was among the earliest and most important influences upon the young poet. When she entered Thakurbari as a young bride, Rabi was eager to make friends with her. He addressed her as Notun Bouthan, and they developed a warm rapport as friends and companions in intellectual pursuits. Like the other Tagore women, Notun Bouthan also enjoyed reading, writing and the arts.

After returning from that first journey to the Himalayas, Rabi found it more and more difficult to put up with the restrictions of school. As his interest in the school routine waned, his poetry-writing flourished. He would find many excuses to avoid going to Bengal Academy. The boys were soon transferred to Saint Xavier's, but the situation didn't really improve for Rabi.

After some efforts, his elder brothers finally gave up on formally educating him. They even stopped rebuking him. One day, his eldest sister Saudamini said, 'We all had such high hopes for Rabi. But he has turned out to be the most disappointing of all.' Rabi realized that his reputation within the family circle was sinking. Even he began to agree with the others that he was unlikely to ever amount to much. The rule of servants had however ended and he had succeeded in his efforts to free himself from the restrictions of school. After enjoying Kalidas's *Kumarsambhava* and Goldsmith's *The Vicar of Wakefield* with his home tutors, he cooled off towards further formal studies and instead devoted his energies to writing poems.

Notun Bouthan shared his love for reading and writing but she rarely showered Rabi with praise. Instead she encouraged, challenged and even playfully teased the young poet to write better. She knew that if she praised him too much, he might grow complacent. She actually succeeded in making him doubt his creative talent. But Rabi did not want to abandon all hopes just because of one person's opinions. Besides, he felt an inner urge to write, which nobody could completely suppress.

Rabi was close to his Jyoti Dada too, but in a different way. The two brothers often shared ideas and collaborated on creative projects. Jyoti Dada guided Rabi in his study of literature. An enthusiastic young man, Jyoti Dada would find joy in encouraging others in creative pursuits. Rabi freely discussed things with him, and never felt ignored because he was only a boy. Jyoti Dada gave Rabi ample freedom to question and experiment. No one else in the family would have dared to offer Rabi such liberty. In the wake of a strictly disciplined childhood, Rabi needed this freedom to grow and overcome his intellectual inhibitions.

During this time, Jyotirindranath's fame was already spreading as a playwright and poet. As a lad in his early teens, Rabi composed a song, *Jwol jwol chita dwigun dwigun*, for Jyotirindranath's play *Sarojini* (1875). This is considered to be Rabindranath's very first song composition. He also contributed songs and poems for some of Jyotirindranath's subsequent works. Rabi was influenced in no small measure by Jyoti Dada's operas, in penning his earliest musical dramas, *Balmiki-Pratibha* and *Kal Mrigaya*. The two brothers had collaborated on the musical scores for these dramas. Rabi loved to hear Jyoti Dada play his experimental musical compositions on the piano. Sometimes he would compose lyrics to accompany Jyoti Dada's innovative scores. Growing up in a talented family, Rabi joyfully took to music as second nature. He never got around to formally studying music though, nor to becoming a trained musician and composer.

Jyoti Dada had ready responses to Rabi's endless questions and arguments. But Notun Bouthan's sprightly repartees were quite different. The duo were thus often at war.

It was fashionable in those days to keep caged songbirds as pets. Notun Bouthan kept a Chinese bird whose warbles charmed everyone. There were many other birds too, all caged in the western verandah of Thakurbari. Every morning, a man came to feed the birds. Grasshoppers and other insects would emerge from his satchel, which also contained seeds of many varieties. Rabi's heart bled whenever he heard sweet songs emerging from cages. 'It's wrong to confine creatures in cages,' he said. 'Don't talk like a schoolmaster,' retorted Notun Bouthan.

Realizing that arguments would get him nowhere, Rabi sought the first opportunity to quietly free some of the creatures. He faced Kadambari Devi's wrath after that, but chose not to reply. Rabi had another ongoing dispute with Notun Bouthan. An enterprising fellow named Umesh collected scraps of lace and fabric from English tailoring shops and patched them together into tacky blouses for the ladies of Calcutta. He would peddle these as the latest high fashion from foreign shores, and the ladies couldn't resist this magic mantra. Rabi pleaded with Notun Bouthan not to patronize his wares. Indian handloom sarees and Dhaka muslins were so much lovelier, he insisted.

Notun Bouthan would tell him to mind his own business, and wear the silly frills anyway. This is how Rabi always lost arguments to her, because she simply held her ground and never bothered to give any lengthy explanations. He would also lose out to her in the game of chess, at which she was brilliant.

Notun Bouthan was an avid lover of literature. She read Bengali books with great enjoyment. Rabi shared her interests and they would spend many happy hours discussing their favourite works. They both admired *Swapnaprayan Kavya*, written by Rabi's eldest brother, Dwijendranath Tagore. Rabi marvelled at the complex structure, with its countless facets and nuances combining to create a wonderful effect on his soul. Although it never occurred to him to try to replicate some of this in his own writing, Rabi was already drawing readers.

Srikantha Babu, the literary critic of a monthly journal, was a devotee and friend of the Maharshi. He wholeheartedly admired and encouraged young Rabi's poetry. Rabi too, was an ardent admirer and disciple of Srikantha Babu's musical talents. The man of letters would take Rabi for outings. He once took Rabi to have his portrait taken at an English photographer's studio. He would take him along when he went to sing and play the sitar at the home of a European missionary too. Srikantha Babu would proudly urge Rabi to sing the songs he had taught him.

Another important association was with Biharilal Chakravarty, whose epic poem was then being serialized in a magazine. Notun Bouthan was delighted by the beauty of his work, and had memorized many sections of it. She would sometimes invite the poet home and had embroidered with her own hands a lovely mat for him to sit on. Rabi got to know the poet during these visits, and earned his affection. Biharilal generously welcomed Rabi to visit his home whenever he wished, and would recite poems and sing songs to the young boy. Rabi hoped that he, too could write such poetry someday.

When Notun Bouthan died in 1883 at the age of twenty-four, Rabindranath was overwhelmed by sorrow. He was haunted by memories of the happy days they had spent together, and at times sought out her presence in the terrace in her roof garden. This sense of loss is touchingly reflected in his song, '*Amar praner porey choley gelo ke*.' Later he dedicated his volume of poetry, *Bhagnahriday* (The Broken Heart), to her. Rabindranath never forgot Notun Bouthan for the rest of his life. He continued to immortalize her in his poems and songs. Her long, lustrous hair and expressive eyes are recurring images in Rabindranath's drawings of human faces.

Rabindranath's novel *Nashtanirh* is considered to be based upon the relationship between Notun Bouthan, Jyoti Dada and himself. In the novel, the character of Amal is based upon Rabi, and Charu is based upon Kadambari Devi. This novel was later adapted into the classic movie *Charulata* by Satyajit Ray, who was a student in Rabindranath's Santiniketan.

Jyotirindranath was a noted literary talent in his own right and a man of adventurous temperament who often took up unusual projects. Jyotirindranath composed plays and operas in the heroic and farcical styles often on historical subjects. His farces, plays on history and musical operas were popular and critically acclaimed. Some of Jyotirindra's plays were translated into Hindi, Marathi and Gujarati. Jyotirindra also translated some French and Sanskrit literary works into Bengali.

The great writer Bankim Chandra Chattopadhyay published appreciative reviews of Jyotirindra's *Kinchit Jalajog* and *Purubikram* in his monthly journal, *Bangadarshan*.

Jyotirindra had an attractive personality and was handsome. He often acted in his own plays.

4 Thakurbari and Its Influences

When Rabi was growing up, Thakurbari was a
powerhouse of artistic, literary and social activities. As
a small boy, he would watch with fascination carriages
arriving at the gates, bringing people into the brightly-
lit mansion. These wonderful people were dedicated
to infusing nationalist idealism into poetry and song,
painting and drama, and even into their style of
dressing. Rabi was particularly fascinated by his cousin
Ganendranath, who composed and produced plays. He
died when Rabi was very young. But the impression
left by the tall, handsome young man who attracted
everyone with his intense energy remained with
Rabi forever.

In those days, people visited Thakurbari not only
to do business, or to pay a courtesy call. People met, as
Rabindranath put it in *Jibansmriti*, 'purely for the joys
of friendship' and freely discussed everything under
the sun. Thakurbari was filled with life and welcoming
laughter. All arrangements and facilities, all the planned
functions, were meant to be shared with everyone.
Though functions were organized on a grand scale in
Thakurbari, there was no snobbery. Even people clad
in shabby clothes could walk in uninvited. They would

receive as warm a welcome as the more eminent and wealthy guests.

Ganendranath's younger brother Gunendranath was another vivacious presence in the mansion. He planned entertainment programmes and produced plays. Once, Dwijendranath had composed a new comedy, which immediately excited everyone in Thakurbari. Rehearsals were held every afternoon in Gunendranath's big reception room. Rabi and the other children would stand on the verandah and peek through the windows, catching wisps of songs and lots of loud laughter. Sometimes, they would catch glimpses of the grown-ups dancing wildly. Rabi could not understand what they were all laughing about. But he felt thrilled that someday, he too would grow up and share these jokes.

Rabindranath never received any prizes in school, except once, a book for good behaviour. In his group of friends, his nephew Satya was the brightest. Once, Satya did very well in an exam and was awarded a prize. As soon as they returned home from school, Rabi jumped off the carriage and ran inside to tell his cousin Gunendranath the good news. Spotting him in the garden, the boy ran shouting, 'Guna Dada, Satya has got a prize!' Guna Dada hugged Rabi close with a smile and asked, 'Didn't you get any award?' 'No, I didn't,' Rabi replied. 'Satya got the prize.' Guna Dada told everyone he met about Rabi's generosity, his joy at Satya's success. Rabi had never dreamt that this was something to be proud of. He was wonderstruck by this unexpected praise. He got a bonus prize for not getting a prize! As a grown-up, he later felt that while it was good to give children gifts, giving them prizes did not make sense. It's best for children to remain open-minded and encouraging towards each other, rather than to be competitive.

Inspired by the artistic atmosphere of Thakurbari, Rabi and the other boys once decided to stage a play. The playwright was none other than Satya. As a boy, Satya was the ringleader of much mischief. Under his guidance, the boys planted some poles in the ground where they usually practised wrestling. They then stuck sheets of paper to the poles and painted colourful pictures for the stage. It wasn't the grandest stage nor the most expertly written script. The boys often forgot their lines or acted out of turn, but they had a lot of fun rehearsing and producing the play.

Innovation and creativity was encouraged at Thakurbari. The Tagore family had imbibed many Western influences, but these were relatively less deep-rooted. Maharshi Debendranath sincerely loved his motherland throughout his life. His influence spread among his family. The steady flame of patriotism was growing deep inside the heart of every Tagore. The era of nationalism had not yet begun in earnest in those days. Many educated people advocated Western learning and culture, and kept themselves aloof from Indian languages and ideas. But Rabindranath and his older brothers were encouraged to use their native Bengali. The Maharshi once received a letter from a relative written in English. He immediately returned it to the sender.

In keeping with this nationalistic spirit, the Hindu Mela was launched in 1867 with the support of the Tagore family. There were exhibitions of Indian arts, crafts and sports, and awards were given to the deserving. The Tagores and others composed patriotic poems and songs, which were recited and sung at the mela. Young Rabi also wrote patriotic essays and poems. Standing under a tree at the Hindu Mela, he read out these passionate childish writings to a rapt audience.

Inspired by the growing spirit of nationalism, Jyoti Dada helped organize a secret nationalist society. Even young Rabi was admitted as a member. Meetings were held in a deserted house in an obscure lane of Calcutta. They were a harmless group. The only frightening thing about their activities was the secrecy. Even their families didn't know where the group was going at midday, and what they were really up to. In a dark room behind bolted doors, they talked in hushed whispers and drew inspiration from mantras of the Rig Veda. In fact, these people were simply looking for an outlet for the mental and physical energy, which was suppressed by the foreign rulers.

The group decided to start factories for making matches and other useful things in the homeland. Members promised to donate one-tenth of their incomes for this initiative. Making matches was, however no simple task. After much experimenting, a few products were ready at last. These matches had value only as proof of the young people's enthusiasm though. The money invested in making one box of those matches, could have lit all the stoves in a village for an entire year. There was another small problem. The matches would not ignite unless they were touched to a ready flame. If only the fire of patriotism could light them, those matches would still be in the market today.

The group members were ever alert to new nationalist activities. Once, they heard that a young student was trying to make a swadeshi weaving machine. They rushed to see it. None of them had any idea if this would be a practical and useful machine. They were idealists driven only by hope and faith. They repaid the loans the student had taken. Then one morning, one of their grey-haired well-wishers, Braja Babu, arrived at Thakurbari with a *gamcha* or towel tied around his head. 'This *gamcha* was woven in our own machine,' he announced, raising his hands and dancing with excitement. Finally, some sensible people joined the group and offered wise counsel to these daydreamers, putting an end to their impractical experiments.

****

During the 18th and 19th centuries, Bengal under British rule experienced enormous social and cultural progress, which historians now call the Bengal Renaissance. These changes resulted not only in an intellectual revival, it also influenced everyday existence. The Tagores played a pivotal role, contributing not only to art and culture, but also to improvements in daily life. They even set new trends in fashion. The dress styles of foreign rulers was no longer considered fit for patriotic Indians. Jyotirindranath proposed nationalist outfits for his fellow countrymen. The native dhoti was impractical for active life, and pyjamas and trousers were unacceptably foreign. So Jyoti Dada invented a hybrid, which in Rabi's opinion put both dhoti and trousers to shame. He folded a length of cloth over the pyjama and tied it as a separate half-dhoti over it. Then he created a hotchpotch of the British solar topi and Indian turban, which nobody in his wildest dreams could call a proper hat.

Jyoti Dada was an extraordinary young man. He wore his weird designs and ventured out in public in broad daylight. Wide-eyed stares from people did not bother him. Rabi felt that many brave patriots could willingly sacrifice their lives for the motherland. But this braveheart, who ventured into the streets of Calcutta in such strange clothes, was to the young boy a rare hero indeed.

Rabi's eldest sister-in-law Jnanadanandini Devi also defied conventions by travelling across the country and even overseas. When in Bombay, she observed the Parsi style of draping the sari. Bengali women in those days were just emerging from the seclusion of purdah. A decent and dignified Indian dress, which they could wear and face the world, was for them a practical necessity. Jnanadanandini Devi taught this Parsi style of sari draping to the ladies of the family, who added their own touches to create the *Thakurbarir sari*. The Tagore family even advertised in newspapers, inviting the high society of Calcutta to a demonstration of the fine art of wearing the sari in the new style. The *Thakurbarir sari* became immensely popular. This is how many Bengali ladies wear the garment even today.

The Tagore men also experimented with clothes, in keeping with their nationalistic ideals. They wore achkans, china coats, *jubbas* and in this way, created their own fashion statement. Maharshi Debendranath was once invited to a musical evening organized by a neighbouring zamindar. The Maharshi was facing a grave financial crisis at that time. So people speculated about what the great man would wear at the high society event. True to his style, he surprised everyone by arriving in a simple outfit set off by a pair of grand pearl-studded slippers! And of course, Rabindranath later went on to create his own signature style of dressing. His long, flowing robes, luxuriant wavy hair and beard and handsome appearance made him stand out at any intellectual gathering.

In 1867 the Hindu Mela was started with the inspiration of Maharshi Debendranath Tagore and his family. The objective was to nurture Swadeshi and promote the development of Indian languages, culture and crafts. Headed by Nabagopal Mitra, this mela was one of the earliest attempts to make people respect India as their motherland. Participants read out poems and speeches on nationalist themes. Gymnastics, wrestling and other traditional sports were also demonstrated. Some of the young participants at the Hindu Mela later became renowned personalities in their own right. Among them was a young man named Narendranath, who went on to gain worldwide recognition as Swami Vivekananda.

5 ✒ Bhanu Singh Thakur Takes Up the Pen

Encouraged by Jyoti Dada and Notun Bouthan, the teenaged Rabi composed new songs and poems. He avidly read anything he could lay his hands on, from Shakespeare's plays in English to popular farces in Bengali, which entertained theatre audiences of those days. Some of these farces, such as Dinabandhu Mitra's play *Nil Darpan* (1860), satirized society and also politics of the times.

In those days, Jyoti Dada managed the family estates in East Bengal. Sometime around 1875–76, he took Rabi there for a visit. The brothers stayed in a secluded, crumbling old house which, in young Rabi's opinion, might very well have been haunted. The house had once belonged to a British indigo planter named Shelley. A tiny village at the meeting point of two mighty branches of the Ganga, from where the Tagore family estates were managed, was named Shelidah after him. Jyoti Dada gave Rabi a pony to ride, and took him tiger hunting.

This secluded and wildly beautiful place was just right for writing. While in Shelidah during this early visit, Rabi experimented with various ideas. Jyoti

Dada encouraged him. For instance, Rabi tried writing poems with ink made from pressed flowers. With his brother's help, he also designed a machine with a cup-shaped wooden sieve managed by ropes and pulleys. The machine was an utter fiasco and that was the last time Rabi tried his hand at engineering or constructing instruments. Although he was a talented composer and singer, he never mastered any musical instruments.

Many years later, Rabindranath would return here during the 1890s to himself manage the family estates. Living in a grand new estate house, he would then grow closer to nature and observe the lives of ordinary villagers first-hand. These experiences inspired many of his later poems and stories.

Although he grew up in a wealthy upper-class family, Rabindranath's writings showed deep humanism and empathy for the poor and downtrodden. 'Postmaster', one of Rabindranath's classic stories, is set in a village much like Shelidah and portrays Ratan, an affectionate orphan girl, with great sympathy. 'Shasti' (Punishment) is another powerful and moving tale in which Tagore shows how the underprivileged are reduced to inhuman conditions by poverty. The story also portrays the strength of the penniless and friendless village girl Chandara, who chooses death with dignity rather than allowing her treacherous husband to use her as a pawn.

As a teenager, Rabi read ancient Bengali poetry with great interest. He could not fully understand the archaic language, but the rhythms fascinated him. He marvelled at the discovery of hidden old literary treasures, and wondered what it would be like to publish his own writing by shrouding it in a similar aura of mystery. Rabi was also intrigued by the dramatic story of the English boy-poet Thomas Chatterton, who had fooled scholars by perfectly mimicking the style of ancient poets. Determined to prove his mettle as a second Chatterton, Rabi jotted down some lines of poetry and showed them to a friend who was sure not to understand a word.

Rabi told his friend, 'An ancient and tattered manuscript has been discovered in the library. I've copied some verses from it written by some old-time poet named Bhanu Singh.' The friend was excited by the discovery of such wonderful lyrics. He wanted to publish them immediately. But when Rabi confessed that he had written them himself, the friend's enthusiasm waned. *Bhanu Singh Thakurer Padabali* (published under the pen name in the family magazine *Bharati* in 1877) was Rabi's first important work of poetry. Rabindranath retained these poems in his collected works, but he did not think they had great literary merit. While the language and style of the poems could be passed off as that of classical poetry, he felt their sentiments were affected and struck a false note.

In 1878, Rabi's second brother Satyendranath, an ICS officer, offered to take him to England. Satyendranath's wife and children were already there, and he was due to join them in September. Concerned about his youngest son's whimsical behaviour the Maharshi approved of the idea. Hopefully Rabi would resume his formal education abroad and train as a barrister.

Meanwhile, Rabi needed to get used to the ways of Western world and its culture.

Satyendranath took Rabi first to Ahmedabad, where he was then working as a judge. There he lived in Shahibagh, the grand house reserved for the judge. It was originally a palace built in the 17th century by Prince Khurram, who would one day become Emperor Shah Jahan. The Sabarmati River flowed along the foot of the palace walls, which supported a broad terrace. While his brother went to attend his duties at court, Rabi explored the vast palace with its many mysteriously empty rooms. Only the cooing of pigeons kept him company, breaking the midday stillness. A large room lined with bookshelves housed Satyendranath's library. A richly illustrated large-print edition of Tennyson's works placed there fascinated Rabi. His grasp over English was not yet as strong as it would become in later years. Tennyson's words and phrases were to Rabi like the cooing of the pigeons—musical and charming, but not fully understood. Rabi's imagination wandered again and again through the beautiful accompanying pictures. Reading works of English literature in this way, Rabi formed a romantic mental image of England. These first impressions would continue to influence his later approach to Western culture.

In his brother's library, Rabi also discovered a collection of Sanskrit poems edited by Dr Haberlin and printed at the old Serampore press. The Sanskrit words were beyond Rabi's comprehension, but their resonant rhythms kept him fascinated. From early childhood, Rabi learned to enjoy books even if he could not understand all the words. He would fill in the gaps with his own imagination.

Wandering alone through Shahibagh palace, Rabi pictured how life would have been in the Mughal times. He would imagine an orchestra playing music night and day from the gallery, while the beat of horses' hooves would echo in the streets. Great parades would be held, with soldiers on horseback brandishing gleaming spears. Terrible conspiracies would be whispered among the courtiers. Princesses would bathe in rosewater fountains in the hamam, their bangles tinkling gracefully. These ideas inspired Rabindranath to pen 'Khsudita Pashan' (The Hungry Stones) a story which would be adapted later by the renowned film-maker Tapan Sinha into a classic movie.

During his stay in Shahibagh palace, Rabindranath composed several fresh and original musical scores to accompany his own lyrics. He had composed songs in the past too, when he and Jyoti Dada had collaborated to produce musical dramas. These new songs marked a stage in the evolution of Rabindranath's unique style, which would one day be known and widely appreciated as Rabindra Sangeet.

Rabindranath's next visit to Ahmedabad happened much later in 1920, at Gandhiji's invitation to attend the Gujarati Literary Conference. By then Rabindranath was an internationally acclaimed writer who had travelled all over the world. He had also been awarded the Nobel Prize for Literature in 1913. Ambalal Sarabhai was a leading industrialist, who played an important role in

India's freedom struggle, hosted Rabindranath during his later stay in Ahmedabad. A strong bond of friendship grew between them.

After a couple of months in Ahmedabad, Satyendranath sent Rabi to Bombay to acquire a different perspective on the West. Rabi stayed with his brother's friend Atmaram Turkhud, a prominent doctor and social reformer sympathetic to Brahmo ideals. Atmaram's sixteen-year-old daughter Anapurna (Ana) had recently returned from England. Ana's westernized and highly sophisticated upbringing was strikingly different from that of other Indian girls her age. Ana and Rabi struck up a warm friendship. She also appreciated the poems he composed.

Rabindranath chose the pen name Bhanu Singh Thakur for some of his early poems because the name sounded like an ancient Vaishnava poet's. It suited his purpose. Also Bhanu, like Rabi, meant the 'sun'. A research scholar who was also a family friend was then in Germany. He was most impressed with Bhanu Singh's poems. He never suspected that they were written under a pen name by Rabi, a boy he knew quite well. The scholar wrote a thesis comparing the lyric poets of Bengal with European literature, praising Bhanu Singh's poetry profusely as the work of a great poet of yore. He even earned his PhD for this thesis.

6 ✒ Voyage to England

In October 1878, Rabi arrived in England expecting it to be a small island filled with people devoted to lofty ideas and culture. The seventeen-year-old lad had imagined that the sweet strains of the poet Tennyson's lyre would resound from every corner of the land. Reality turned out to be rather different. Rabi was comfortable enough spending some months with his brother Satyendranath's family. He was in many ways like most teenagers, enjoying music and playing pranks with friends his own age. He would entertain his little niece Indira and nephew Surendranath by singing popular English songs. He also often sang a Hindi song in a comical style, leaving the children in splits.

Rabi was enrolled in a British school in Brighton, and spent some time there. However, he made little progress towards becoming a barrister. Satyendranath was dissatisfied, and sent him away to London. Rabi found London cold, bleak and forbidding, but he also enjoyed attending occasional parties and dances, and meeting new people. Rabi once cut an impressive figure in the grand dress of a Bengali zamindar at a fancy dress ball, but felt hurt when the ladies shied away from him because of his false moustache. He also enjoyed singing in groups and summoning ghosts at planchettes with the daughters of his landlady, Mrs Scott. Rabi admired the vitality and boldness of some of the English girls he met. He was also critical of some English women's affectations and preoccupation with their physical beauty though. In a letter home, Rabi wrote that he felt pity for such women, since they seemed to have no independent lives of their own. Although they were beginning to gain access to education, its effects were barely noticeable. They could read novels without the aid of a dictionary, but as yet showed little capability to achieve more.

As Rabi mingled with the British, he found them to be a mixed lot. He got along well with some of them like Mrs Barker, in whose home he stayed briefly as a paying guest. But Mr Barker was rough and surly, and Rabi felt embarrassed and helpless witnessing the man's nasty behaviour towards his wife. When he lived with the Scott family, Rabi was touched by the kindness of Mrs Scott, who treated him as a son. Her daughters also showered him with rare warmth.

On the other hand, Rabi's experiences with an English doctor and his brother were far from pleasant. Both of them looked down upon Rabi as a 'complete ignoramus'. They would stop by shop windows to explain that photographs were taken by machines, and not drawn by human hands. They would explain what wonderful inventions watches were. The brothers thought Rabi was some sort of savage because he did not subscribe to the Ten Commandments, and did not know what a muff was.

These were not the only things about England that disappointed Rabi. He used to think that in England, bookstores were as necessary and important as butcher's shops. While strolling through the streets of London, he was surprised by the profusion of wine shops, shoe stores, tailors, butchers and toyshops. But he hardly came across any bookshops. As for the English working classes, he observed the mechanical rush in their struggle for existence.

Rabi was also put off by the affected snobbery of his own countrymen in England. His eldest brother Dwijendranath described these anglicized Bengalis, who tended to blindly ape Westerners, as *ingabangas*. Rabi himself was quite different, and did not wish to be like them. He went on to satirize *ingabangas* in many of his later stories.

Rabi also noted the fundamental differences between Indian classical music and Western music, which to him seemed poles apart. Rabi felt that European music seemed to be intertwined with the everyday life of Europe, so that the lyrics of their songs could be as varied as life itself. If Indians tried to put their own native melodies to the same variety of uses, the tunes would lose their significance and become quite absurd. Indian melodies were meant to transcend everyday life and carry listeners deep into emotions, such as pity and devotion, to reveal the core of their being. There was no room for the busy man of the world in Indian music, in Rabi's opinion. Indian songs celebrating the rains did not try to imitate the sound of falling raindrops. Instead, they attempted to portray the emotions people associated with the rainy season. The main objective of Indian music is to correctly and artistically render the melody, and all efforts were focused towards this. Our connoisseurs were content if they heard the song. In Europe, they went to hear the singer. Rabindranath later made this observation in his autobiography, *Jibansmriti*.

During this first visit to England, Rabi also observed the proceedings in the House of Commons from the Visitor's Gallery. He was surprised by the rowdy behaviour of some British MPs, who did not hesitate to hurl insults at each other. Ireland was in those days subjugated by the British, and Rabi noticed how the Irish MPs seemed to be sidelined by the others. Only nine or ten MPs participated in a debate on Indian affairs. The remaining members entered the chamber only when it was time to vote. The votes of the MPs were usually decided by party policies, Rabi inferred. He felt that the Conservatives were 'blindly dogmatic.' To him the Liberals seemed more reasonable. He later described them, in a letter home, as people who 'do what they consider right. That is why they have such differences of opinion among themselves.' Rabi was very impressed, though, by the speeches made in Parliament by W.E. Gladstone, who would one day become the prime minister.

Meanwhile, Rabi attended classes at University College, Cambridge. He particularly enjoyed Henry Morley's lectures on English literature. He also struck up a warm long-term friendship with his classmate Loken Palit, who later entered the elite ICS and served as a magistrate in the interior regions of Bengal. Soon, Fate would pull them in different directions and Rabi would never complete his studies. His brother Satyendranath's tenure in England was about to end, and he was returning to India with his family. Rabi's father, the Maharshi, instructed his youngest son too, to return home in 1880, although according to earlier plans, Rabi was to have acquired higher educational qualifications in England.

From a young age, even before his first visit to England, Rabi dreamt about an ideal synthesis or union of Eastern and Western values and ideas. European thought is more action-based, he felt, and revolves around freedom, practical intelligence and acquisitiveness. Indian thinking is imaginative, more profound and stresses upon placing the good of others above self-interest. Penning down his ideas in an early essay, Rabi marvelled at the wonderful, almost perfect character that could be created by a synthesis of these two streams of thought. Despite the annoying and uncomfortable situations he faced at times during his first visit to the West, this ideal of synthesis became strengthened in Rabindranath's mind. He continued to uphold his faith in this ideal well into his old age, even into the days when India's freedom struggle began gathering momentum against the exploitative British rule.

After returning from England, Rabindranath wrote prolifically from 1880–1883. He composed not only poetry, but wrote musical dramas, a novel and essays. He also continued to write interesting and thoughtful letters to people close to his heart, such as his niece, Indira Devi. He would continue to write with such variety and profusion for the rest of his life. The collection of poems, *Bhagnahriday*, appeared shortly after Rabindranath's return home. Later at a more mature age, Rabindranath thought these early compositions were trivial and childish, and not fit to be included in his collected works. However, the collection did earn appreciation from readers, and considerable literary prominence for the poet. In Calcutta's literary circles, Rabindranath came to be known as the Bengali Shelley and also the Lisping Poet. This embarrassed Rabindranath, who later wrote, 'My attainments were few, my knowledge of life meagre and in both poetry and prose the sentiment exceeded the substance.'

Soon after Rabi's return from England, he and his brother Jyotirindranath resumed composing music with renewed enthusiasm, experimenting with both Western and Indian melodies. Rabindranath's creative collaboration and joyful camaraderie with Jyoti Dada and Notun Bouthan flourished. The widely appreciated musical drama *Valmiki-Pratibha* was composed during this period. Some of the melodies for the songs in this opera were composed by Jyoti Dada, and while many songs were adapted from the Bengali kirtan tradition, some were also adapted from English tunes, to which the brothers added their own touches of originality. With Jyoti Dada's encouragement, Rabi set about to write, compose songs, and even act and sing in his own operas, with all the energy and aplomb of a twenty-year old.

In 1882, Rabindranath published a major collection of poetry titled *Sandhya Sangeet*. A few months after this book was published, Rabindranath attended a wedding where Bankim Chandra, the towering figure of Bengali literature, was also present. When the host came forward to garland Bankim Chandra, he declined the honour and said that Rabindranath deserved the garland because of his wonderful poems in *Sandhya Sangeet*. Rabindranath cherished this spontaneous compliment from the great man for the rest of his life

In 1883, Rabindranath accompanied Jyoti Dada, Notun Bouthan, Satyendranath's wife Jnanadanandini and her children to Karwar in present-day Karnataka, where Satyendranath was then posted. Rabindranath was moved by the natural beauty of the landscape of this coastal town in the Western Ghats. Fragrant sandalwood trees grew on the hillsides, guarded by forts which had been built by the Maratha leader Shivaji. The pristine beaches, lush forests and towering hills inspired his creativity. *Prakritir Pratishodh* (Nature's Revenge) a verse drama, was composed here. While the inspiration came spontaneously, Rabindranath took care to craft his poems to perfection. Bubbling emotions did not necessarily give rise to good writing in the heat of the moment, he felt. The hues of poetry are best expressed with the paintbrush of memories. The present has the power of immediacy. It must, however, be controlled to allow the imagination to find its rightful expression. This Rabindranath held true for all forms of creation. He felt that the artist needs to achieve some amount of objectivity and distance from raw, immediate emotions in order to create enduring art.

In 1882, the Maharaja of Tripura wished to honour Rabindranath. The Maharaja's wife had recently died, and in his bereavement, he had found solace in the poems in *Bhagnahriday*. This admiration laid the foundation of a lifelong relationship between Rabindranath and the rulers of Tripura, who would help financially at a vital stage in the setting up of Santiniketan.

Later in 1927, the then Maharaja of Tripura even sponsored Rabindranath's visit to Bali and Java. According to a recently-released telegram dated 28 June 1927, Rabindranath had requested the last Tripura king, Bir Bikram Kishore Manikya Bahadur, for financial help. Funds were required to sponsor the travel of the renowned painter and sculptor Dhirendra Krishna Deb Barman, on a trip to Java along with Rabindranath. Such a tour would give Deb Barman a fantastic opportunity to develop his career as an artist. At Rabindranath's request, the Maharaja promptly offered the then princely sum of Rs 3,000 for the trip.

Dhirendra Krishna Deb Barman was himself a member of the Tripura royal family and he went on to become principal of Kala Bhavan in Visva-Bharati, the university set up by Rabindranath at Santiniketan. There are several other instances of Rabindranath's close links with the royal family of Tripura. His novel *Rajarshi* alludes to the life of the Tripura royals in ancient times.

7 Marriage

On 9 December 1883, twenty-two-year-old Rabindranath was married to a girl of eleven. Her name was Bhabatarini, an old-fashioned name even in those days. She was the daughter of an employee of the Tagore estates, and came from Jessore in East Bengal, from where several other Tagore brides also hailed. Rabindranath had never met her before marriage, relying completely upon the choice made for him by his elders. Bhabatarini was renamed Mrinalini (lotus blossom) by Dwijendranath. Rabindranath's elder sisters-in-law had also had the poetic names Jnanadanandini and Kadambari conferred upon them after marriage.

Rabindranath's wedding took place in the Jorasanko Thakurbari. It was a simple affair. The groom wore a family heirloom set of silk clothes and a grand shawl. He played pranks even on his wedding night. According to tradition, a game of dice had to be played. Rabindranath deliberately misplaced the pieces. Finally an aunt became annoyed and ordered him to sing. So Rabindranath sang, 'I'm charmed by your beauty' to the shy little bride huddled under her veil. The song had been composed by his sister Swarnakumari Devi.

This match was not an unusual one for the family, or for the times in which they lived. The marriages of Rabindranath's older brothers and sisters had been arranged in a similar manner. His brothers had also married child brides much younger than themselves. Rabindranath and Mrinalini Devi formed a fruitful partnership, and had five children. Mrinalini Devi proved to be a solid and unobtrusive pillar of support to her husband. She gladly left the comforts of Thakurbari to stand by his side and help him realize his dream of founding an ideal educational institution at Santiniketan. She even contributed her jewellery to finance the university. She took interest in the work there, especially in the children's section. She died at a young age in 1902, shortly after the founding of Santiniketan. The poet was left heartbroken at his loss. Some of Rabindranath's poems from this time express his deep sorrow. One such poem, 'Smaran', is included in the English version of *Gitanjali*.

Like many young girls of her times, Mrinalini Devi had received very little education up to the time of her marriage. Soon after the wedding, she was sent to stay in Central Calcutta with her much older and highly accomplished sister-in-law Jnanadanandini, who had just returned from England. Mrinalini Devi was admitted to Loreto House, a famous convent school for girls. She did not sit with other students in class. Arrangements were made to teach her separately. She also picked up the intricacies of refinement and etiquette from Jnanadanandini, who was the queen bee of Calcutta's *ingabanga* (Bengalis exposed to English culture) society. An Loreto, Mrinalini Devi was taught English, music, Sanskrit and how to play the piano.

Like the other Tagore women, Mrinalini Devi became involved with the arts. Initially, the new bride was too shy to speak much, especially because she had a noticeable East Bengal accent. But soon, she acquired confidence enough to perform in plays with poise and skill. She also translated the Ramayana, and with Rabindranath's guidance and encouragement, compiled and wrote down some Bengali folk tales. Her daughter Mira remembered Mrinalini Devi as a good oral storyteller. Rabindranath's nephew, the famous artist Abanindranath Tagore, found the story 'Khirer Putul' in Mrinalini Devi's diary after her death. His children's classic of the same name is based upon this tale.

Mrinalini Devi was also an excellent cook. When cultural gatherings were held in Thakurbari, Rabindranath requested her to prepare special menus. Her culinary skill was widely appreciated on such occasions. To tease her, Rabindranath would try out unusual recipes himself, and often create a mess.

During this period when a new chapter of his life began with his marriage, Rabindranath also suffered a severe personal setback. Only a few months after his wedding, Notun Bouthan committed suicide. Rabindranath was shell-shocked at the loss of one so near and dear. The reasons for Notun Bouthan's suicide were never made public. It remains a mystery to this day.

This tragedy had a lifelong effect on Rabindranath. But as a self-disciplined creative artist, he did not allow the clouds that had gathered in his heart to cast a permanent gloom on his writing. Rather, his personal tragedies and sorrows intensified his perceptions and added more depth and nuance to his work.

During this time, Rabindranath dedicated himself to perfecting his art. *Manashi* (Lady of the Mind), a collection published in 1890, was his best and most widely appreciated work so far. The young 'lisping poet' Rabi had earlier written sentimental poems, whose depth and substance did not come up to his aspirations. Now the grown-up Rabindranath was blossoming into a poet of powerful emotions, who would express himself on diverse themes.

The beauty and harmony of nature was a major source of inspiration for Rabindranath. He saw the natural world as a state of harmony. The fearsome and clashing aspects of nature, he felt, are like individual notes of a song. They combine with the beautiful elements to make a harmonious whole. In the poem 'Sindhutaranga' (Waves of the Ocean) in *Manashi*, he writes on the terrible destructive forces of nature:

The sharp white terrible mirth of brute Nature.
Eyeless earless rootless loveless,
The mad forces of Evil

This poem was inspired by a shipwreck on the Bay of Bengal during a storm, in which over 700 innocent pilgrims had perished.

Some other poems in *Manashi* are humorous or satirical drawing attention to social problems such as child marriage. Thus in the poem 'The Wedding Night', the bridegroom, a strapping young man, makes an eloquent amorous speech to his bride. The beauty and romance is lost on the tiny child bride, who only whimpers and says, 'I am going to sleep with my nurse.'

In 'Duronto Asha' (Wild Hopes), Rabindranath pokes fun at those Bengalis who talk big and think they can do anything if they only try. What pulls them down is lack of initiative and meek submission to their ordinary fate. 'If only I would be an Arab Bedouin!' cries an young man in the poem, dreaming of a life of wild adventure. But he is in reality rooted to his drab life playing cards and smoking hookah with other 'rice-fed, milksop offspring of Bengal.'

Rabindranath himself was quite the opposite of the milksop portrayed in his poem. He loved travel and adventure. Once, he even planned to explore the entire stretch of the Grand Trunk Road from Calcutta to Peshawar in Afghanistan, roughing it out by riding bullock carts or trekking. His father, a great traveller, encouraged this plan, but somehow this expedition never took place.

Rabindranath felt that literature is an important source of knowledge. From early childhood, people crave for new experiences. This gives birth to myths, fairy-tales and legends. Literature helps people explore themselves and the common human condition in varied ways and to discover both beauty and ugliness. At one time, Rabindranath was certain that the main objective of literature was to create beauty. Later he realized that the range of literary and artistic expression covers much more than conventionally beautiful subjects. A deep sense of joy is the proof of beauty. Through literature, we can safely widen the scope of our experiences and our minds can accept knowledge and joy from even the most insignificant things of life.

A deep sense of spirituality runs through Rabindranath's poetry. He was open to the ideas and philosophy of the Baul mystic folk singers and Sufis of Bengal, and Hindu Vaishnavism and Buddhism. There is no similar concept of a supreme universal soul in Buddhist thought. However, Lord Buddha also thought it was shallow and dangerous to stress upon individual differences. He taught his followers to have sympathy for everyone in this world, to love others without feeling enmity or the desire to do harm. The Buddhist concept of Nirvana can be compared in several ways with the Hindu concept of Mukti. The philosophy of the Upanishads influenced Rabindranath the most. Inspired by ideas from these philosophies, he created a distinct spiritualism of his own.

Rabindranath was born into the Brahmo Samaj, a movement which revived the Hindu religion based upon what the ancient sages had taught in the Upanishads. Maharshi Debendranath Tagore had first introduced the child Rabindranath to these philosophical texts while on a journey to the Himalayas. The Upanishads aim to understand the divine power behind this ordinary material world, and the relationship between the creator and creation. This supreme divine power pervading the universe is the Brahman. This immortal and infinite force is within each of us, and unites us all on a fundamental level. When we understand this truth, we become more open and accepting, and consider humanity as one large extended family. This understanding can connect human beings with the ties of selfless love.

Rabindranath tried to understand reality through human emotions, and through poetic vision and feeling rather than knowledge. The beauty of nature, the wide blue sky, gurgling streams, floating clouds and the song of birds; the beauty of the face of a loved one; the warmth and affection in some human relationship—it was through such direct human emotional experiences and not through any philosophical theory that Rabindranath found the interconnectedness of human beings, and the relationship between humanity, nature and the infinite.

Rabindranath felt that people needed to reach out beyond their limited selves and love and empathize with fellow human beings. Also, people should be in harmony with nature and the universe, in order to extend themselves beyond narrow, selfish concerns and participate in the joy of divine creation. The objective is not simply to know about the mechanical aspects of this world and make use of it. The ultimate aim is to open our minds and hearts to love the beauty of nature, and the goodness of humanity as a part of this natural world.

Rabindranath diversified his talent as a writer in the years after his marriage and the death of Notun Bouthan. During this period, he also translated English poetry into Bengali. He even edited an illustrated children's magazine named *Balak* (The Boy), which had been started by his sister-in-law Jnanadanandini. Rabindranath discovered that he enjoyed this new challenge. Later on, he edited other magazines.

Jnanadanandini wanted the young boys of the Tagore family to showcase their writing in *Balak*. She also knew that the magazine could not sustain itself with just their work. So she asked Rabindranath to take up the responsibility of not only editing, but also writing for *Balak*. From 1886–87, the magazine serialized Rabindranath's novel *Rajarshi*, based on a historical incident about the Tripura royal family, whom he knew well as admirers of his poetry.

The story behind *Rajarshi* is interesting. Rabindranath had just visited Deoghar. The train back home to Calcutta was very crowded, and he could not rest. So he tried to pass the time by trying to think of a new story. But this effort made him doze off. He dreamt of a little girl crying out with fear at the sight of blood from a sacrifice on the steps of a temple. She turned to her father, who pretended to be angry with her and tried to hush up the matter. Yet he too, was deeply moved. This dream inspired *Rajarshi*. Rabindranath had a deep understanding of the hearts and minds of children.

This found expression in his poems revolving around childhood. Rabindranath wrote the poems in *Shishu* (Child) during his stay in Almora in 1903. These lovely poems were meant to entertain his young children after the untimely death of their mother.

During this period after his marriage, Rabindranath also entered public life for the first time. He wrote and lectured on controversial topics, such as child marriage. With the passing away of Keshub Chandra Sen in 1884, the Brahmo Samaj had lost a capable and charismatic leader, who had lead the way in social and religious reforms. Rabindranath was appointed secretary of the 'High Church' wing of the Samaj, which was at the time headed by his father. Rabindranath's efforts to infuse new ideas into the Brahmo Samaj were however, opposed by the more orthodox members. They disagreed with his arguments that Brahmos were a branch of the wider Hindu philosophical framework, and that theirs was not an independent religion.

What even the most orthodox Brahmos did like about Rabindranath were his devotional songs. Even Swami Vivekananda, the great Hindu revivalist, appreciated them and sang them to his guru, Shri Ramakrishna Paramhansa. While these religious songs won the approval of the Brahmos, they were much heavier and gloomier in tone compared to the rich and varied songs, the much loved and appreciated Rabindra Sangeet, Rabindranath later went on to write.

The Tagore family had been searching for sometime for a bride for Rabindranath. The ruler of a princely state in the Madras Presidency had a suitable daughter. Jyoti Dada escorted Rabindranath there to meet the girl. The brothers were presented to two ladies in the palace. One was a striking beauty and the other was plain. The brothers were naturally pleased at the sight of the lovely lady, only to learn later that she was the bride's stepmother.

8 ✒ Shelidah

In 1891, Rabindranath shifted to Shelidah, now in Bangladesh, to manage the family estates. He stayed there for ten years, and tried in practical ways to improve the lives of the poor villagers under his charge. He spent much time travelling on the Padma River in his boat, going from village to village to supervise work on the estates. He came in close contact with the rural poor, felt a deep empathy for their trials and tribulations, and appreciated their innate qualities as human beings. It was during his stay in Shelidah that Rabindranath began writing short stories. His experiences and observations of human nature, his contact with the lives of ordinary people and their joys and sorrows, enriched his stories and novels.

In the estate headquarters in Shahzadpur, Rabindranath would enjoy ruling over a spacious building called the *kuthibari*, which was all for his own use. Every morning he would throw open all the doors and windows, and allow the light and air to bring in the essence of the outside world. He felt the mood and urge to write here as nowhere else. The heat, quiet and solitude of the afternoons, the warbling of birds and the cawing of crows would work their magic during the unlimited leisure time and carry Rabindranath into the world of imagination. It was on one such balmy afternoon that the idea of 'The Postmaster' (1891) took over his thoughts. This was one of Rabindranath's earliest stories, and was later made into a moving film by Satyajit Ray in 1961. Rabindranath once met a real postmaster, upon whom he based the disenchanted and weary young man from Calcutta in the story. The real-life postmaster read the story and recognized himself, for though he was not from Calcutta, he shared the fictional postmaster's urge to escape from the constraints of rural life.

Rabindranath's short stories were unusual for his time. These pioneering tales connected with the soul of Bengal—the mischievous children; loving mothers and sisters; poor, hard-working villagers and other ordinary people. In those days, other noted writers from Bengal were composing fanciful and romantic stories about the heroic adventures of princes and feudal noblemen. These stories by Rabindranath's contemporaries were based on history and legends, and were far removed from day-to-day reality. Rabindranath's stories revolved around simple, true-to-life characters such as the village postmaster, the little orphan girl Ratan, and villagers such as Chidam and his proud and beautiful wife Chandara, who suffers a tragic fate. His tales brought to life the realities of rural Bengal. He also wrote stories about urban folk, and characters from different social backgrounds, but all his narratives were realistic depictions of people and situations of those times.

Critics have sometimes accused Rabindranath of portraying a poeticized and romantically stylized account of rural life. How could a man from a privileged upbringing ever understand the lives of poor, ordinary people? Rabindranath himself was surprised by such censure. After all, he had spent many years on Bengal's rivers in his houseboat, closely observing and interacting with the villagers. He wrote from what he saw, and based his stories upon impressions from these direct experiences. Therefore, he felt there was realism in his stories, and it was wrong to dismiss them as fanciful and lacking in substance. Rabindranath did write some highly imaginative stories such as 'The Hungry Stones', but such stories were also based on acute observations of reality. Rabindranath portrayed vibrant images of life in Bengal in his short stories. His poetic imagination deftly blended his perceptions and ideals with what he realistically observed to create unforgettable impressions. He did not see the need to seek out clever shortcuts, but treated his subjects with natural ease and feeling, finding both happiness and sorrow and finally a sense of peace. These touching stories, enriched with Rabindranath's gentle wit and social criticism, continue to be widely read and appreciated to this day.

Shelidah is a relatively modern name. Its old name was Khorshedpur. Before the Tagores of Jorasanko acquired the village in the middle of the 19th century, there stood a *kuthi* built by a planter named Shelly. A deep *daha* (whirlpool) was formed there at the meeting point of the Gadai and Padma River, and hence the village came to be known as 'Shelley-daha'. This mutated by popular usage into 'Shelidah'. While Shelidah was a secluded region in Bengal's heartland, it was only half a day's journey from the bustle of Calcutta by train or boat. This gave Rabindranath the best of both worlds. He had ample peace and privacy in the *kuthibari* and in his houseboat to write many poems, stories and songs. Indeed, this period of stay in Shelidah was one of the most artistically productive phases in Rabindranath's life. He wrote the songs of *Gitanjali* during this period and also began their English version, which would earn him the Nobel Prize in 1913. The English *Gitanjali* is not an exact literal rendering of the Bengali *Gitanjali*. Rabindranath added new and original touches to the English version of his song offerings to make it a special collection of literary gems.

Apart from writing, Rabindranath took his administrative duties very seriously. As a just and upright zamindar who truly cared for the welfare of his tenants, he set up a system parallel to the government courts for dispensing justice among the rural people under his charge in Shelidah. Disputes between villagers were first heard by village headmen. Their verdicts could be appealed against and taken to a court of five headmen from various parts of the zamindari estate. From there, the final court of appeal was with Rabindranath himself. He received special recognition from the colonial government for creating this system. It worked very well for many years.

These years of work in the villages convinced Rabindranath of two things. He strongly felt that instead of waiting for the government to do things for them, Indians must learn to help themselves. He also came to the conclusion that the key to India's advancement lay in uplifting its villages. Acting true to his beliefs, he founded several small business ventures in the 1890s. Poet and visionary that he was, Rabindranath could not match the business acumen of his father and grandfather. These enterprises failed. Nevertheless, India's first modern patriotic movement, the Swadeshi Movement of 1905, took root from this point. Rabindranath was one of its champions.

In Shelidah, Rabindranath also grew to love the natural beauty of Bengal's landscape: emerald fields of paddy, lush green plants growing on the rich alluvial soil, the vast blue sky and the life-giving rivers, the sweet songbirds and other living creatures. He developed a deep affinity with the Padma River. It flowed in an undercurrent of recurring images in his poetry, in collections such as *Shonar Tori* (The Golden Boat) published in 1894.

Far from the crowds and bustle of Calcutta and faced with the secluded, timeless grandeur of nature, Rabindranath felt more introspective. He would immerse himself in the inner world of his thoughts and lose track of time. He would watch the river flowing to the sea, and listen to the melodious and plaintive *bhatiali* songs sung by the boatmen. Their voices would rise and fall with the rhythmic beat of the waves, reflecting the ups and downs of the human condition. The haunting lyrics of these folk songs, created and passed down through generations of boatmen, expressed the longing of the soul for the eternal. Themes of love, human pain and sorrow, and joy in daily life predominated in these lovely songs. *Bhatiali* songs influenced Rabindranath. This was reflected in *Gitanjali* and his other poems and songs.

While living in the peaceful rural setting of Shelidah, Rabindranath would also visit Calcutta frequently, interact with family and friends, conduct business, attend to publishing, give lectures and otherwise enjoy the social and intellectual stimulation offered by the big city. Eminent people from Calcutta also occasionally came to visit Rabindranath in Shelidah. Among them were the scientist Acharya Jagadish Chandra Bose and the playwright Dwijendralal Roy.

For the better part of his tenure in Shelidah, Rabindranath's wife and children remained in Calcutta, coming to Shelidah for occasional visits. In 1898, they moved from Calcutta to settle in Shelidah. His children Bela (12), Rathindranath (10), Renuka (7), Mira (4) and Samindranath (2) were growing up. He did not want them to suffer from the unhealthy and deficient education system, which he felt to be the source of many problems in India. Rabindranath took up the task of educating his children himself. From 1898 to 1901, they all lived together as a happy family.

The children had teachers trained by Rabindranath to give them lessons in English, maths and sanskrit. The teachers lived in the estate house. The British teacher who taught the children English was quite eccentric. He shared his quarters with thousands of silkworms, whom he referred to as his children. Rabindranath personally taught his children Bengali. He let them read freely from books of their choice. Sometimes he would share with them the poems he was composing, discussing and analyzing them in detail.

Bhatiali is a traditional form of folk music of Bengal. These are folk songs traditionally composed and sung by boatmen on Bengal's numerous rivers. Rivers played a vital role in the lives of Bengalis, sharing in their joys and sorrows. The waterways were also vital for transport and commerce, acting as major routes for transporting people and crops.

The word Bhatiali comes from *bhati*, meaning the river bank, and *bhata*, meaning ebb tide. These songs voice the sorrows, joys and longing of the people of *bhati* regions. The melodious songs were originally composed and sung by boatmen, who pined for their loved ones while undergoing lonesome journeys to the endless sea. In a wider and symbolic sense, the lyrics also expressed the longing of the soul for the infinite and eternal.

9   Santiniketan: The Abode of Learning

As he neared forty, Rabindranath thought more about moving to Santiniketan and founding a school there, far from the distractions of Calcutta. His father provided for a school in the trust deed of his ashram and gave his blessings. Towards the end of 1901, Rabindranath and Mrinalini Devi moved to Santiniketan in Birbhum district, West Bengal, with their children. Rabindranath would consider this place his home till the end of his life.

Although many trees had been planted here after the Maharshi first chose this place for meditation many years ago, this region was hotter and less fertile than the river-crossed landscape of Shelidah. But Santiniketan had its own natural beauty, which found reflection in Rabindranath's writing. In 1901, Rabindranath Tagore set up a school at Santiniketan based on the ancient gurukul system. In the beginning, there were only five students, including Rabindranath's eldest son Rathindranath.

Tagore stressed on simple living in Santiniketan. Students lived an austere life in huts. Classes were held in the open air, and the food was plain. This made the upper-class people of Calcutta regard the school as an eccentric and impractical concept, and shy away from enrolling their children there.

Having suffered when young from restrictive and unimaginative methods of learning, Rabindranath realized all too well the need for a child's mind to blossom and grow in a healthy and uninhibited way. He was particularly concerned about the trend of imposing English on Indian students at the cost of neglecting their mother tongue and traditional culture. He noted with mounting concern the tendency of educated Indians to blindly ape British manners, speech and customs. Rabindranath felt that Indians who had received Western education, relied on borrowed ideas without truly understanding their significance. Rabindranath felt that education should be liberal, accessible to students in their own native language, and free from narrow sectarian constraints. However, while he was against colonialism and the mindless imposition of English language and culture on young students, he did not reject Western ideas and ideals. He appreciated their liberal and critical spirit; urging young people to think on their own and to ask questions. He felt that interaction with outside forces was necessary to maintain our own vitality, rousing us from the inertia of formal, time-honoured intellectual habits.

Rabindranath disapproved of the artificial imposition of foreign education upon Indian students. He felt that such training slowed down the creative process in young students, and hampered original thinking. As such, it became a burden upon young minds. Rabindranath advocated the strengthening of our own culture, not by resisting Western culture, but by accepting, mastering and assimilating it into our own. He felt that foreign education must nourish us and broaden our intellectual horizons, rather than slow down our intellectual growth. These ideas and ideals went into the founding of Visva-Bharati University.

Creatively expressing his worries, Rabindranath wrote a satire about a parrot's education, 'Tota Kahini'. In the story, a king ordered a parrot to be educated. The pundits stuffed it with so much studies that the helpless and confused bird choked to death. Rabindranath strived to make his own university the opposite of this. He wanted to expand the imagination and critical thinking of young people and to encourage them to ask questions rather than parrot traditional learning.

Rabindranath felt that the Western emphasis on science raised the danger of progress at the cost of making moral compromises. This could be balanced by educating the masses, and by encouraging the liberal arts. Human capacities needed to be nurtured side by side with scientific progress. He felt that education must remain close to the roots of human personality. He sensed that British culture was repressing feelings and emotions. That was one of the reasons why he chose to have classes in the open air and close to nature in Santiniketan.

Santiniketan had originally been called Bhubandanga after Bhuban Dakat, a local bandit. In 1862, Maharshi

Debendranath Tagore halted here while on a boat journey to Raipur. The serene natural scenery, rows of chatim trees and date palms charmed him. He purchased nearly seven acres of land and named the spot Santiniketan (abode of peace). Santiniketan became a spiritual centre where people from all religions were invited to join for meditation and prayers. The Maharshi founded an 'ashram' here in 1863. Chhatimtala continues to stand today in the Viswa-Bharati campus as the Maharshi's meditation spot.

It took Rabindranath many decades of focused effort to develop Santiniketan, first as a school, and later as a university. In the initial years, he even had to sell his wife's jewellery to keep the fledgling project going. Meanwhile, Rabindranath suffered a series of tragedies in his personal life. He lost his wife in 1902, when she was barely thirty years old. Left to care for his heartbroken young children, Rabindranath suffered another bereavement when his daughter Renuka died of tuberculosis a year later, at the age of twelve. It was as though the little girl wasted away pining for her lost mother. Through the rest of his life, Rabindranath continued to be battered by sorrow, as he watched his other children die one by one. His youngest child Samindranath died in 1907 at the age of eleven. His eldest daughter Madhurilata (Bela) passed away in 1918, aged thirty-two. Of his five children, only Rathindranath (1888–1961) and Mira (1894–1969) survived their father.

When Rabindranath's father passed away in 1905 at the age of eighty-seven, it was like the fall of a great banyan tree that had sheltered the family. The Maharshi had already divided the estates among his four sons. After his death, the brothers set up their own establishments, and nobody remained in No. 6 Dwarkanath Tagore's Lane, the Thakurbari where Rabindranath had grown up. Only Rabindranath's nephew Abanindranath, the illustrious artist, still lived in the adjoining house with his two brothers.

After his father's death Rabindranath steeled himself to soldier on, excelling in composing new works and winning accolades in India and worldwide. His personal sorrows imbued him with a deeper philosophical understanding, and added more depth and nuance to his work. By 1904, his omnibus which included his novels, stories, plays, songs, essays and letters, had sold over 10,000 copies. Such large sales of his works did not bring him a great deal of wealth. What it did achieve though was to establish without doubt that Rabindranath was the country's best known and most acclaimed living writer.

Finances had always remained a major concern in building up Santiniketan. As Rabindranath's reputation as a writer grew, he travelled around the world, interacting with writers and intellectuals. Winning the Nobel Prize in 1913 boosted his burgeoning reputation. Rabindranath's audience expanded greatly, and he used this popularity to mobilize support for the cause of Santiniketan. During World War I (1914–1918) and its aftermath, Rabindranath's voice gently yet firmly spoke of peace in a world shattered by violence. The poet travelled to distant lands projecting understanding and amity as the most desired objectives of humanity. He also tried to raise funds for his international centre of learning, a university, which would help forge these bonds of understanding among diverse people spread across the globe.

The idea for Visva-Bharati University was conceived in California in 1916, while the world was in the throes of a terrible war. The foundation stone was laid in 1918, and Rabindranath hoped that the institution would live up to its Sanskrit motto, which translated to 'Where the whole world meets in one nest'. It would offer India's intellectual wealth to everyone, and also accept the best from other cultures. Rabindranath wanted to create a unique centre in Asia where seekers of knowledge would feel freed from the spirit of contempt and hatred, which divided westerners and Asians. Visva-Bharati adopted a constitution of its own and was formally inaugurated on 23 December 1921.

Three departments formed the core of Rabindranath's new university, and they remained the strongest as the institution evolved. The department of fine arts (Kala Bhavan) was managed by the eminent artist Nandalal Bose, who was Abanindranath's pupil. The department of music (Sangit Bhavan), was managed by Dinendranath Tagore, Rabindranath's eldest brother Dwijendranath's grandson. Rabindra Sangeet formed a major section of this department. The other core department was that of Indology. It revolved around studies of Buddhist literature, Vedic and Classical Sanskrit, Pali, Prakrit, Tibetan and Chinese. This department was a major attraction for foreign scholars.

Rabindranath the artist

Kala Bhavan was meant to give a fresh thrust to Indian art. Under the able guidance of Nandalal Bose, students were encouraged to break free from convention and let their imaginations soar. Rabindranath himself was a talented painter. Though he is better known as a poet and writer, his paintings outnumbered his songs. Even as a young boy, he liked to sketch. In 1924, while writing *Purabi*, he created unusual doodles on the pages of his manuscript. Some of these fanciful illustrations were on the borders of the pages, while others covered over changes in the writing. Lacking formal training in art he experimented and produced striking results by playing with lines and colours. He relied more on drawing with a pen, using ink and watercolours. He preferred dark greens, violet and blue over red. Rabindranath spoke about the beauty of nature and highlighted the ideal of tranquility in his poems and songs. But his drawings and paintings were mainly dark and mysterious studies. He sketched strange, murky creatures and eerie scenes which continue to intrigue viewers. In his art, he often portrayed fanciful and stylized animal forms. These can be interpreted as omens of the evils that he feared would threaten the modern world. When asked about the meaning of his darkly striking pictures, Rabindranath said that their latent significance was for the viewer to experience and feel. He likened love to art, because both were inexplicable.

While Rabindranath was travelling in France in 1930, some art critics saw his paintings and advised him to exhibit them. The first public exhibition of Rabindranath's works was held in Paris in May 1930, at the Gallerie Pigalle. In the same year, more exhibitions followed in England, Denmark, Sweden, Rome, Germany and Russia. They earned great public acclaim. His artworks were also later exhibited in the USA and Canada. A collection of over 1,500 of his paintings are preserved in Visva-Bharati. Many other paintings are part of the collections of important museums around the world.

Santiniketan is also the home of the Rabindrik Nritya. Rabindranath absorbed ideas from all over the world and blended them with concepts from Indian classical dance to create a unique dance style. The dance form shows traces of Kathak, Manipuri and Odissi, among its many influences. It is rife with emotion and was created to complement Rabindranath's songs and dance dramas. This classical based dance form is considered free style, since it has no set movements. In many classical dances, there are special fixed movements designated to depict things, such as rain or wind. In the Rabindrik style, the movements are varied and depend upon the emotion and ideas conveyed by the song. They are very delicate, fluid and evocative.

Rabindranath also pioneered the concept of *Bhav-Nritya*, which used physical movements to bring out the emotions and ideas of the accompanying song. In Rabindranath's time, conservatives felt that dance was meant only for women of questionable character. They believed dance performances to be a threat to social morality. Rabindranath worked to liberate Indian dance from such a narrow view. He stood his ground against orthodox Bengali scholars, who opposed the public performances of his dance dramas. Path-breaking American dancer Isadora Duncan (1877–1927) was among the eminent foreign artists and intellectuals, who spent some time studying Rabindranath's approach to dance. Her genius inspired other modern performers of her time to create their own individual styles.

Santiniketan went on to produce several acclaimed alumni. Among them was the world-renowned film-maker Satyajit Ray and Indira Gandhi, who later became prime minister of India. Ray considered the three years he spent at the university to be the most fruitful years of his life. Santiniketan opened his eyes for the first time to the splendours of Indian and Far Eastern art.

Many years later, in 1982, Indira Gandhi recalled her life-changing experience in Santiniketan. She said, 'I was so interested in all the aspects of Gurudev's personality, not just as a poet—he was even painting at that time—but in his vision in general. So many things [that] are fashionable today but were unheard of in those days, were all there in Gurudev. For example, the environment and concern for the environment.' As a young woman, she observed and absorbed the multifaceted activities and way of life in Santiniketan. These values became a part of her inner life. In Santiniketan, she felt that she gained most from the 'ability to live quietly within myself no matter what was happening outside. This has always helped me to survive.'

Santiniketan is also home to Amartya Sen, the 1998 Nobel Prize winner in Economics. Rabindranath even gave Amartya Sen his unusual name. Sen completed his schooling in 1947 from the open-air school in Santiniketan. He went on to study Economics in Presidency College in Calcutta and returned to Visva-Bharati as Visiting Professor for a year in 1983. According to his mother Amita Sen, 'Tagore is his *dhrubatara* (guiding star) and Santiniketan is the place where he comes to seek peace.'

Rabindranath's vision brought about many innovations in Santiniketan. He saw the need for setting up Sriniketan, an institute for rural reconstruction aimed at educating poor village boys and girls and involving them in the process of shaping them into future leaders, who could guide their rural communities to solve their own problems. Sriniketan was founded in 1922 at Surul, a few kilometres away from Santiniketan. It stood for freedom from poverty and ignorance, and the vision of a better life facilitated by modern knowledge, collaboration and self-help. It was formally inaugurated on 6 February 1922 with Leonard Elmhirst as its first director. It also took over the work of training in handicrafts already begun by Silpa Bhavan in Santiniketan.

When Gandhiji visited Santiniketan in 1940, Rabindranath entreated him to take charge of maintaining the school, which he felt was the most important work of his life. He said to Gandhiji, 'Accept this institution under your protection, giving it an assurance of permanence if you consider it to be a national asset. Visva-Bharati is like a vessel which is carrying the cargo of my life's best treasure . . .' This was shortly before Rabindranath's death in 1941. Today, more than seventy years after Rabindranath's passing, the institution continues to uphold the ideals with which it was set up. However, Santiniketan has today incorporated characteristics such as a formal syllabus and examination system, which make it more like other universities.

Rabindranath loved nature and created a space filled with greenery around the campus. He introduced several festivals glorifying the beauty of changing seasons. These celebrations were not confined within narrow religious boundaries. Everyone was free to participate.

Vriksharopana and Halakarshana are festivals celebrated in August for planting saplings and preparing the land for cultivation. The campus is enlivened by music, dances and chanting of Vedic hymns to invoke nature's fertility and regeneration. Varshamangal celebrates the splendours of the monsoon rains in August. Silpotshava is celebrated in September and showcases local handicrafts. Pous Utsav is celebrated on the seventh of Pous to commemorate the Maharshi's initiations into the Bramho religion and the foundation day of 'Brahmacharya Ashrama'. The day begins with prayers at Chhatimtala, and cultural functions continue for three days. This festival became an important event in

Rabindranath's time. It was a meeting ground for urban and rural people. Rural artisans brought their products, such as lovely batik printed cloth, skillfully embossed leather bags, pottery, paintings and other artefacts to display and sell at the fair. Urban participants displayed new things produced in the cities, which rural people could learn about and buy. Basantotsav is celebrated to mark the festival of Holi. Spring is welcomed with music and dance. The teachers and students greet each other by smearing coloured *abir* powders.

10 ✒ Where the Mind is Without Fear

Rabindranath grew up with a deep love and respect for his native land, its people, culture and natural beauty. His early upbringing, education in his mother tongue and participation in gatherings such as the Hindu Mela, all laid the foundation for his intense patriotism. As he grew up, his poetic and artistic spirit blossomed with inspiration from the world around him. He was deeply involved in the reformist movement. As the first Asian to receive the Nobel Prize for Literature, he was known to the world as a mystical poet. But this was only one aspect of his multifaceted genius. His vast body of writing expressed not only his creativity, but also revealed the social, political and critical aspects of his brilliant mind.

During his years in the family estates in Shelidah, Rabindranath came in close touch with ordinary people and sensed their troubles and feelings as human beings. His deep concern for his fellow Indians from all sections of society came alive in his narratives. Very few short stories had been written in Bengali before his time. Rabindranath was a pioneer not just of the literary form of short stories, but also for its focus on ordinary human beings. Rabindranath was not an aggressive revolutionary. He felt that true and lasting change could only come through a change of heart, and not through lectures or the use of force. He artistically expressed these views in his short stories and novels, as well as through his other writings. Rabindranath also wrote many well-reasoned essays, in which he expressed his unique, complex and interesting opinions on the political and social order of India and her place in the rest of the world.

In 1905, the Swadeshi Movement swept up a storm of patriotic feeling throughout Bengal. The immediate trigger was Lord Curzon's announcement that Bengal would be divided into two states. This partition was widely considered by Indians as an attempt to stifle growing nationalism in Bengal. People everywhere protested through mass meetings and rural unrest. The Swadeshi Movement also called for the boycott of British goods.

The British rulers proceeded with the partition despite popular agitation. The emotional fervour of the Swadeshi Movement touched a chord in Rabindranath. He passionately opposed this division of his beloved motherland, and even became one of the leaders of the Swadeshi Movement for a brief period. In later years though, he grew disillusioned with its shortcomings, and distanced himself from the Swadeshi Movement. This disenchantment found expression in his novel *Gharey Bairey* (The Home and the World). He supported patriots who worked toward their goals without resorting to violence, and who were willing to go to prison in support of their ideals. But he disapproved of insensitive leaders who manipulated the emotions of the masses. He was also shocked by the communal divisions which led to violent riots after 1907.

In 1911, British India's capital was relocated from Calcutta to Delhi, and East and West Bengal were reunited. The British rulers did this to appease sentiments and to make it easier to govern the region. This calmed the people for a while. But the Muslims of Bengal seethed with resentment because they felt they stood to gain from Partition. The final division of Bengal happened in 1947, churning the region with violence. West Bengal was allotted to India, while East Bengal now belonged to East Pakistan, and later to Bangladesh in 1971. Rabindranath loved his motherland deeply, and was pained at her predicament. His heartfelt emotions found expression in his writing.

The ongoing animosity between Englishmen and Indians also pained Rabindranath. He felt that this happened partly because Indians had initially approached Europeans without thinking deeply, or asking enough questions about their motives. Such a flawed approach often invited insults or injuries, which then hurt the pride of Indians in their own race. This made Indians instinctively rebellious. They then became withdrawn, and refused to accept the positive values Europe had to offer. Rabindranath felt that if Indians approach Europeans in this blindly emotional manner, they would gain nothing. Instead, Indians needed to recognize, accept and make their own the genuine principles and ideas of Europeans. This would broaden their outlook and strengthen their characters. In this way, Indians could acquire more wisdom and more effectively demand their rights.

To Rabindranath, patriotism and nationalism did not mean proving superiority over other nations with sheer military power. Indians would make a grave mistake, he felt, if they paid back Europeans by returning malice and wrongs in their efforts to be free from foreign rule. He clearly perceived the flaws as well as strengths of Western culture and thought. While Europeans were capable of being humane and creative, Rabindranath felt they could also be vicious and oppressive, feeding upon the resources of other nations in order to promote their narrow self-interest. He saw too clearly the darkness and destruction the West brought upon humanity through World War I.

Rabindranath also saw the danger in extreme approaches to the West. Indians tended to either blindly ape the West, or treat with unreasonable suspicion everything the West had to offer. Therefore, he urged Indians to approach the West in a balanced frame of mind. Rabindranath accepted from Western culture the spirit of liberalism, humanism and critique. He urged young people to ask questions and not blindly accept anything as irrefutable truth. He also appreciated the rich artistic and cultural heritage of the West; its spirit of scientific inquiry and justice. Rabindranath also felt that it was imperative to 'convince the West that the East has its contribution to make to the history of civilization.' Rather than rejecting Western civilization and isolating themselves, Indians needed to have a deep association with the West.

Santiniketan was based upon these ideals. Rabindranath also devoted his efforts towards building up a National Council of Education. He worked on the syllabi of courses, gave a series of lectures on literature and helped in raising funds. This gradually evolved into Jadavpur University in the 1950s.

Rabindranath put his patriotic ideas into action not through politics, but through his sincere personal efforts to better the lives of ordinary Indians. He was angry at the injustice and insult heaped upon his motherland by foreign rulers. But he wanted to turn this anger into positive efforts to improve the lot of his fellow countrymen. He attempted to establish some swadeshi businesses in the 1890s. He also promoted Indian journals such as *Bangadarshan*. He boldly and lucidly expressed his views on current affairs and social issues.

In 1903, the Viceroy of India, Lord Curzon, arranged a grand durbar or court in Delhi to celebrate the coronation of King Edward VII and Queen Alexandra as Emperor and Empress of India. Maharajas came with their courtiers from all over India, dressed in rich robes and fabulous jewels. A tented city sprung up over a barren plain, and a temporary light railway track was laid out to bring crowds of spectators from far-off places. This township had its own post office with special stamps, and a police force with unique uniforms. It even had its very own hospital and magistrate's court. Dazzling fireworks, bright lights and magnificent dance performances added to the glamorous show. True to his nationalistic principles, Rabindranath denounced Lord Curzon's durbar as a showy and wasteful display of opulence.

Concern for his downtrodden countrymen was always uppermost in Rabindranath's mind. He suggested that a band of workers be mobilized to deliver knowledge on improving sanitation and agricultural practices to villagers through songs, magic lantern shows and plays. These workers could discuss with the villagers about what they really wanted for improving educational facilities, roads, water supplies and other matters. The Indian political leaders who lived in the cities wanted to rouse the villagers to rebellion against the British. But Rabindranath felt that they did not care enough about improving the lives of the rural poor. So he took up his own developmental projects on his estates. He had already set up a system of dispensing justice there. During the Swadeshi Movement he had promoted a project that covered nearly seventy thousand people from 125 villages in the Tagore estates. Under this project, villagers elected representatives from among themselves, who planned and executed undertakings for developing their own villages. New schools, roads, health care facilities and other projects for public good were launched. The elected village officials proposed and collected taxes by themselves from their fellow villagers. This money, along with funds from the estate, was used to improve facilities in the villages. The society worked so well that it continued even after the estates were taken over by the government of East Pakistan after Independence in 1947.

Rabindranath cherished the hope that his descendants would use their education and capabilities to help improve life in the villages of the country. In 1905, he sent his son Rathindranath to Urbana Champaign in the USA to study agricultural science. Until then, the Tagores and other leading families of Bengal had traditionally sent their sons to Cambridge and Oxford for higher studies. 'R.N. Tagore Jr' became one of the first Bengali students in the USA. In 1907, Rathindranath's brother-in-law Nagendranath Gangulee (husband of Rabindranath's youngest daughter Mira) also went to the USA to study agricultural science.

Rabindranath established an agricultural bank in his estates to help free poor villagers from the clutches of greedy moneylenders. The bank became very popular and loan sharks were driven out of business. The only problem was collecting enough money to lend to farmers. Rabindranath borrowed money from his friends, since he did not have much funds of his own at that time. In 1913, the Nobel Prize brought him a huge sum of Rs 1,10,000. Rabindranath donated this money to the Santiniketan School and suggested that it should be invested in the agricultural bank.

The bank thus had more capital to lend to needy villagers. This also brought the school a steady income from interest.

Meanwhile, British oppression was on the rise. On 13 April 1919, British commanders ordered the merciless killing of hundreds of unarmed people, who had gathered for a peaceful protest meeting at Jallianwala Bagh in Amritsar. News of this terrible carnage slowly filtered in despite press censorship. Rabindranath was deeply disturbed. Most other leaders hesitated to take a public stand against the killings at that time. On 30 May, Rabindranath composed a letter of protest to Lord Chelmsford. At the end of this letter, he expressed his wish to give up the knighthood which he had been awarded four years ago after winning the Nobel Prize. He wrote that such 'badges of honour make our shame glaring' when other Indians had been humiliated in such an inhuman manner. He wished to stand by the side of his long-suffering and downtrodden countrymen as one of them, and not as someone with the special distinction of knighthood.

Nobody had ever wanted to voluntarily give up their knighthood before. Lord Chelmsford sought the advice of his officials, who felt this showed great disrespect towards the King of England. Lord Chelmsford himself felt that relieving Rabindranath of his knighthood would give him and his nationalist cause more publicity. It might be interpreted as an admission by the British of their mistaken policy in the Punjab. Therefore, the British rulers never revoked the knighthood. Officially he remained Sir Rabindranath, though he gave up his claim to that honour.

As the freedom struggle gained momentum, it was but natural that the greatest patriots of those times would grow closer. Rabindranath and Gandhiji came to know each other through their mutual friend C.F. Andrews, a British missionary and poet. Both Rabindranath and Gandhiji were true patriots who worked tirelessly to better the lives of their downtrodden countrymen. The two towering personalities had deep respect and affection for each other. In 1919, Rabindranath addressed Gandhiji as 'Mahatma' or 'noble soul' for the first time in a letter. This name soon became popular nationwide. Rabindranath always proudly projected Mahatma Gandhi as the spiritual soul of India. Gandhiji, for his part, addressed Rabindranath as 'Gurudev'.

The two great men shared a unique bond which remained strong till the poet's death. Their ideas, personalities and attitudes though, were often in disagreement. 'No two persons could probably differ so much as Gandhi and Tagore!' Pandit Nehru once wrote. Rabindranath was an intellectual, an artist and an admirer of beauty. Gandhiji was a man of action, austere and practical by temperament. Rabindranath believed in progressive, modern ideas, in scientific advancement and in the universal brotherhood of humanity. Gandhiji gave less importance to science and technology. He was a politician and a leader of mass movements.

Rabindranath and Gandhiji sometimes offered each other frank criticism and although they did not always agree with each other's ideas, they gave each other due respect. Rabindranath had reservations about Gandhiji's non-cooperation movement, and 'long hesitated to welcome it to my heart.' Spinning the charka remained a bone of contention between Gandhiji and Rabindranath. Rabindranath disagreed with the Mahatma's view that all patriotic Indians had to spin khadi. But Gandhiji continued to uphold the symbolic significance of spinning.

After a visit to Santiniketan, Gandhiji observed that students did not need servants, sweepers or cooks. He believed that they should manage these chores themselves, along with their studies. Rabindranath readily accepted Gandhiji's suggestion, and the new self-help system was launched on 10 March 1915. It was observed as 'Gandhi Divas' in Rabindranath's ashram.

Rabindranath's efforts nurtured Indian's growing nationalist spirit in many ways. His songs were a source of inspiration for patriots, lending a melodious voice to their ideals. In 1906, Rabindranath wrote *Amar shonar bangla* as a rallying cry for opponents of Partition. In 1972, this became the national anthem of Bangladesh. It is interesting to note that the song had been composed against the Partition of Bengal. But East Bengal, which later became Bangladesh, came into existence only as a result of Partition.

In 1909, freedom fighter Ullaskar Dutta was sentenced to death by the British for being a terrorist. During his trial, he sang a patriotic song written by Rabindranath. Everyone in the packed courtroom, including the European sergeants, listened to his sonorous voice in rapt silence. The *Bengalee*, a daily newspaper, carried a moving report along with an English translation of the song, *Sarthak janam amar* (Blessed is my birth for I was born in this land). This was one of the earliest published English translations of a Tagore song.

Rabindranath also wrote 'Jana Gana Mana', which is now India's national anthem. It was sung for the first time at the meeting of the Indian National Congress in Calcutta in 1911, for which it was officially composed.

Rabindranath's composition *Ekla chalo re* (If they answer not thy call, walk alone) roused millions of souls across India during our freedom struggle. This was Gandhiji's favourite song, and it embodied the spirit of his satyagraha movement.

Where the mind is without fear and the head is held high:
Where knowledge is free;
Where the world has not been broken up into fragments
by narrow domestic walls;
Where words come out from the depth of truth . . .

This is how one of Jawaharlal Nehru's favourite poems by Rabindranath begins. Rabindranath's immortal words beautifully convey the dream Nehru shared with him for the country they both loved.

Rabindranath remained a true patriot till the end of his days. In 1931, two political prisoners were shot dead, and twenty others were injured by guards at Hijili in Bengal. While the British authorities justified the violence, nationalists raised a cry of protest. Rabindranath had kept a distance from politics and avoided public rallies since 1905. However, the feeble elderly poet now appeared in public meetings to protest the killings. He firmly supported the nationalists in denouncing the 'homicidal callousness' which had resulted in the deaths of the victims.

The political climate in India was growing more turbulent. Gandhiji was arrested shortly after returning from the Second Round Table Conference in London. The British rulers were growing harsher against him and the freedom movement. They announced the Communal Award in 1932. According to this new British plan, Hindus, Muslims, untouchables and some other communities would have separate electorates in the constitutional reform of India. Gandhiji began a fast-unto-death protesting this move. Rabindranath agreed with the Mahatma that such a reform would help Britain divide the nation with the help of certain factions of scheming Indians. Despite being old, weak and overwhelmed by sorrow in his personal life (his only grandson Nitindranath had just died from tuberculosis), concern for his motherland remained uppermost in Rabindranath's thoughts. He felt deeply pained when communal forces threatened to divide India.

Rabindranath's liberal views on nationalism and universal oneness of humanity were open to misinterpretation by some extreme elements in the freedom movement. In October 1916, he narrowly escaped being assassinated by a faction of Indian revolutionaries in San Francisco. They probably mistook him for an agent of the British rulers of India. Meanwhile, many other revolutionaries took inspiration from Rabindranath's patriotic songs and speeches.

11 ✒ The Nobel Prize

In May 1912, Rabindranath set sail for England along with his son, daughter-in-law and a friend belonging to the royal family of Tripura. During the long voyage, Rabindranath would sit in a deckchair and continue to work on translating his poems into English. In London, Tagore's poems made a strong impression upon the literary world. Rabindranath cut a striking figure with his flowing robes and large, soulful eyes, as he read out his poems and sang at gatherings. The Western world perceived him as a mystical wise man from the exotic East; dreamy, dignified and serene.

William Rothenstein was among the first to be excited by Rabindranath's manuscript. The two men formed a strong attachment and Rothenstein introduced Rabindranath to the great Irish poet W.B. Yeats, and to other eminent writers, artists and intellectuals. Rothenstein also helped to get *Gitanjali* published in England by the India Society, and later by Macmillan. Rabindranath acknowledged the debt by dedicating the book to Rothenstein.

Yeats too was deeply moved by Rabindranath's poems. He carried the translated poems with him for days, reading them in trains, in omnibuses and even in restaurants. He often had to put away the manuscript because he did not want strangers to see how much the poems emotionally affected him. He perceived that Rabindranath's imagination reflected a vast and rich civilization and culture, which was at that time completely unknown to Western people. And yet, Yeats felt moved not simply because of the unusual qualities of Rabindranath's poetry, but also because his work reflected universal human truths.

William Butler Yeats went on to win the Nobel Prize for Literature in 1923, ten years after Rabindranath. Ireland in those days was ruled by the British, just like India was, and the two nations shared common problems. Yeats, like many other Irish writers and intellectuals, was searching for ways to establish a new literary tradition for his beloved country, based on its heroic past. Rabindranath's writing and personal friendship had an impact on Yeats and his efforts to establish the role of poets and poetry in Ireland's evolving national culture.

Rabindranath also considered Yeats to be an outstanding poet, and was impressed with the image of Yeats as the 'national' voice of colonial Ireland. Rabindranath himself had a similar image as a 'national' poet in a land ruled by the British. They rose from comparable conditions, though one poet belonged to the East and the other to the West. The two great writers saw each other as the voice and poetic spirit of their respective peoples.

Ezra Pound, another great poet of the twentieth century and a friend of Yeats, also met Rabindranath and appreciated his work. Ezra Pound was, in those days, the foreign correspondent of Chicago's *Poetry* magazine. He arranged to get some poems by 'the very great Bengali poet Rabindranath Tagore' brought out by his magazine in the winter of 1912. Those were Rabindranath's first writings to be published in America.

Yeats and Pound teamed up with William Rothenstein to become Rabindranath's strongest supporters. They promoted Rabindranath's poems throughout the Western world, drawing worldwide recognition for the poet from Bengal. Their enthusiasm affected many in Western literary circles. Soon, other great contemporary writers such as England's Poet Laureate Robert Bridges, Andre Gide, Saint-John Perse, Hart Crane and Robert Frost also became admirers of Rabindranath. British poet Wilfred Owen was actually carrying with him a book inscribed with lines from Rabindranath, when he was killed in battle in World War I.

Meanwhile, a few prominent Western intellectuals and writers such as Bertrand Russell, Bernard Shaw and T.S. Eliot, were less enthusiastic in their response to Rabindranath. Yet the universal appeal of Rabindranath's poems had by now been clearly established. *Gitanjali* was an instant bestseller in England. Six successive reprint editions came out within six months to meet the great demand.

Rabindranath's popularity soon spread across the Atlantic. In October 1912, he sailed for America and settled in Urbana, Illinois. His son Rathindranath was completing his doctoral thesis at the university there. Urbana was then a quiet place in the US. The effects of Rabindranath's acclaim in London had not yet reached here. Even then, local people were eager to hear him speak. Rabindranath delivered many lectures at the University of Chicago and also at Harvard University. These were published in 1913 as *Sadhana: The Realisation of Life*. People already began conjecturing that someday, Rabindranath would win the prestigious Nobel Prize.

Rabindranath returned after this round of foreign tours to his abode of peace. 14 November 1913 was a typically tranquil day in Santiniketan, where the news of the great honour arrived by cable. The young students went wild with joy. Many of them did not quite know what the Nobel Prize was, but they understood that their beloved Gurudev had achieved an amazing feat. The students marched around the ashram singing their school song 'Amader Santiniketan'. When Rabindranath emerged from his chamber to greet his pupils, the youngsters threw themselves down and touched his feet. Rabindranath felt very embarrassed by all the homage. Later, the boys made a bonfire and celebrated late into the night.

Rabindranath was the first non-westerner to receive the Nobel Prize for Literature. Rabindranath could not attend the award ceremony in Stockholm. Accepting this great honour, Rabindranath sent a brief telegram which was read by the British Chargé d'Affaires, at the Nobel Banquet on 10 December 1913. Rabindranath finally received the award from then governor of Calcutta in January 1914.

Rabindranath outshone other brilliant and renowned rivals such as Tolstoy, Ibsen, Zola, Strindberg, Shaw, Thomas Hardy and Yeats in winning this great honour. The Nobel Prize was awarded for the *Gitanjali*. People all over the Western world acknowledged the idealism and poetic perfection of this work. There was also some criticism when this honour was given to an Asian for the very first time. As a result, Rabindranath's image grew beyond that of an individual poet. The award was perceived to represent Western recognition of the so-far undermined people of Asia. Rabindranath drew the attention of Western intellectuals to the vibrancy and immense potential of Asia and her people. As a great world personality, Rabindranath came to be considered far and wide as the 'universal man', defender of public liberty, voice of India and the living symbol of her culture.

Rabindranath was unassuming by nature, and feared that he would get no peace henceforth. His heart sank at the prospect of being feted and being made a public show. As the days passed, his ordeal continued. He was compelled to attend functions, listen to oratory in praise of his genius, and make modest speeches of his own. He was forced to leave behind the verdant fields of Shelidah and the tranquility of Santiniketan, and confine himself to the family mansion in Jorasanko, Calcutta.

Rabindranath was most upset by insincere reactions to his great honour. Among the crowds that thronged to greet him in Calcutta, there were several noteworthy people who had earlier censured Rabindranath in writing and in speeches. The same persons, who had once disapproved of him for being manipulated by the West, were now praising him for earning laurels from the West.

Along with global acclaim came criticism, often without basis. A rumour held that the poet Yeats had rewritten *Gitanjali*, and glory had wrongly been given to Rabindranath for what was largely Yeats' work. In fact, Yeats' major contribution was in selecting the best and most suitable poems for the collection. While Yeats did offer valuable advice for revisions, the translations were done mainly by Rabindranath himself.

As soon as Rabindranath and his companions arrived in London in June 1912, a disaster almost occured. Rabindranath's group had to take the underground train from Charing Cross Station to their hotel in Bloomsbury. They had never travelled in underground trains before, and were confused by London's complex tube system. They jostled through crowded platforms, trying hard to keep track of the many trains speeding in different directions. The next day, Rabindranath wanted to go through his manuscript of the *Gitanjali*. His son helped him search everywhere, but the precious manuscript had vanished! They soon realized that in the rush, Rabindranath had lost the briefcase containing the only handwritten manuscript of his translated poems. Fortunately for Rabindranath and the world, the briefcase with its priceless contents was later found deposited at the Left Luggage Office.

12 ✒ A Citizen of the World

Rabindranath often felt restless and travelled frequently to many parts of India and the world. This wanderlust continued into his old age. Even in his last days when he was unable to travel long distances, he would shift from house to house within Santiniketan itself. Travel enriched his experiences. It inspired his brilliant mind to continue to produce new and more beautiful writing; poetry, drama, stories, essays and songs.

Rabindranath had travelled abroad several times since his first trip to England as a teenager. He had already gained eminence as a writer in the USA, England and other European countries. The Nobel Prize made him more prominent and appreciated all over the world, and especially in Asia. He was invited to visit and give speeches and lectures in many countries. He used these opportunities to express his world view, and to mobilize funds for Visva–Bharati.

When Rabindranath first arrived in Tokyo, Japan in 1916, he was greeted by an excited throng of nearly 20,000 people at the railway station. Reporters and photographers swarmed around him as cameras flashed. Yasunari Kawabata, who would become the second Asian to win the Nobel Prize for Literature in 1968, was then a small boy. He was struck by newspaper photos of the sage-like poet, with long, flowing hair, beard and robes, who seemed to the little boy to be like some ancient Oriental wizard.

Japan in those days was a rising Asian power. The country had never been subjugated by Europeans. The Japanese were at that time following the European model by bringing about land reforms, encouraging industrialization, and strengthening their armed forces. In 1895, Japan had waged war against China and won a resounding victory. In 1905, Japan had defeated Russia. This was the first military victory by an Asian nation over a European one. In 1910, Japan became even bolder and took control of Korea.

Deep in his heart, Rabindranath believed that 'Asia is one.' He sincerely hoped that Japan would not forget its ancient culture by blindly imitating the West. He felt that this deviation from its true inner spirit would ruin Japan. He felt that it was Japan's mission to take the lead in spreading the ideals of the Orient. He wanted to bring together the two hemispheres of East and West, which were drifting farther apart every day.

Soon, the initial enthusiasm of Japanese leaders cooled towards the poet. Rabindranath's first speech in the country was reported in their newspapers under the jarring headline: 'Tagore Curses Civilization.' Rabindranath realized that the Japanese were nervous about his ideals, because they thought idealism would weaken their morale, and that they needed to be strong at all costs. The Japanese felt that diplomatic cunning and the use of weapons of brutal power should not be shunned, in order to strengthen and enrich their own nation.

In 1920, Rabindranath visited France. He found the country delightful, and the people warm and welcoming. In 1921, Rabindranath received an enthusiastic welcome in Germany. A million kilos of paper had to be imported from America to print enough German editions of Rabindranath's books to meet popular demand. His German publisher Kurt Wolff recounted how Rabindranath had impressed his countrymen with his striking presence, and his interest in their nation and its heritage. He posed simple, precise, intelligent questions about the costs of war, of the future of German literature, and other aspects of German life and culture. Rabindranath's speeches and conversations with German intellectuals revealed the breadth of his learning.

Rabindranath's visit to China in 1924 was a chance to renew the historic links first forged by Buddhist missionaries from India thousands of years ago. More than the details of Chinese politics or ancient relics and ruins, Rabindranath was interested first and foremost in meeting students, intellectuals and artists. He wanted to find out what the men and women who would build the new China were thinking about.

In those days, some Chinese leaders perceived India as a 'lost' country, which had been subjugated by foreigners since Mughal times. They felt that India had no native leaders capable of ruling the entire country, and that Indians were losing in their efforts to obtain equality and dignity. However, Rabindranath did achieve considerable success in building bridges with the help of culture and literature. He befriended several Chinese writers, and many of his works were in the course of time translated into Chinese. A high point in Rabindranath's trip to China was his visit to the Forbidden City to meet the former emperor. He was the first foreigner to receive this rare honour.

Rabindranath's sojourns also took him to distant South America. While he was travelling in Japan, Rabindranath had received an official invitation to visit Peru on the occasion of the centenary celebrations of the country's victory over their Spanish colonial rulers. Rabindranath accepted the invite and planned to proceed from there to Mexico. The representatives of Peru and Mexico promised to donate a large sum for Visva-Bharati.

In 1924, Rabindranath met an extraordinary Argentinian lady, Victoria Ocampo. She was widely read and a patron of the arts. Victoria Ocampo had written many essays, critical studies, memoirs and translations. She also published the literary magazine *Sur* (South), which launched the careers of great writers like Jorge Luis Borges. Rabindranath, then aged sixty-three, was exhausted by all his travels. He fell seriously ill, and Victoria Ocampo offered to accommodate him as a guest in her mansion until he recovered. Rabindranath usually did not write new poems when he was travelling outside India. But during his stay in Argentina, he composed many poems, which were later published in the widely appreciated work, *Purabi*. He dedicated this collection to Victoria.

By this time, Rabindranath was a well-known literary figure in South America. Spanish translations of his works by Juan Ramón Jiménez, a poet who went on to receive the Nobel Prize for Literature in 1956, had made Rabindranath and his writings widely popular throughout the Spanish-speaking world. In Chile, Gabriela Mistral, the first Latin American to win the Nobel Prize in Literature in 1945, and Pablo Neruda, winner of the Nobel Prize in Literature in 1971, were clearly influenced by Rabindranath's writings. Mexican poet Octavio Paz recounted how the youth of his times eagerly read Rabindranath's poems. Paz himself went on to win the Nobel Prize for Literature in 1990. Rabindranath's work left its mark on all these brilliant South American writers.

In the course of his travels, Rabindranath also interacted with several international political leaders. He even had an interesting encounter with the Italian dictator, Mussolini. In the 1920s, many eminent people such as T.S. Eliot, Bernard Shaw, W.B. Yeats and Winston Churchill respected Benito Mussolini and Italian Fascism. This was long before the evils of Fascism had revealed themselves. The dark clouds of World War II had not yet begun to loom over the world. In 1926 Rabindranath received an invitation from Mussolini to visit his country. Rabindranath received a grand welcome in Italy, and Mussolini told the poet that he had read every one of his books in Italian. Rabindranath also met the king, and watched one of his own plays being acted out in Italian. Despite the initial warm reception Rabindranath was piqued by the contradictory nature of Mussolini. The Nobel laureate was also troubled by the signs of increasing repression and brutality already visible in the Fascist government. Soon, his relations with Italy and Mussolini soured, and he distanced himself from the dictator. Mussolini later sided with Hitler in World War II (1939–1945). His country was defeated, and Mussolini was assassinated.

Rabindranath later visited many other countries such as Austria, Norway, Sweden, Denmark, Czechoslovakia, Hungary, Rumania, Bulgaria, Greece and Egypt. Everywhere he went, he was highly respected and appreciated by leaders, intellectuals and ordinary people.

In 1930, Rabindranath met the scientific genius Albert Einstein several times in Berlin and in New York. Albert Einstein (1879–1955) was a German-born physicist who developed the general theory of relativity, which revolutionized Physics. He received the 1921 Nobel Prize, and is known today as the father of modern physics. He was also a renowned humanist.

These two brilliant men exchanged philosophical ideas with the help of an interpreter. Einstein believed that truth existed independent of mankind. The moon, for example, was true and real, whether people looked at it or not. Rabindranath on the other hand, believed that one could never go beyond humanity in all that one knew and felt. To clarify Einstein asked, 'If there were no human beings any more, the Apollo Belvedere (a famous classical marble sculpture from Italy) would no longer be beautiful?'

'No,' Rabindranath responded with conviction. According to him, truth could be realized only through human perception.

In 1930, Rabindranath visited Soviet Russia, a vast country spread across both Asia in the east, and Europe in the west. Rabindranath made an indelible impression of the Russians. His paintings were exhibited in Russia, and Russian translations of his writings were deeply admired. After the Revolution of 1917, a sea change was taking place there under the Communist rulers. Rabindranath visited factories and schools and saw for himself how Russia had empowered the dispossessed. He was particularly impressed by a visit to a Pioneer Commune in Moscow in 1930. He felt that suffering humanity now had a nobler vision of itself on the world stage. He noticed how social divides between the haves and have-nots were crumbling. Poor Russian labourers were now sending their children to good schools. Ordinary citizens visited art galleries in Moscow, where only the wealthy and privileged could enter before the Revolution. Rabindranath hoped that the Russian example could motivate and benefit his own motherland.

Rabindranath's visit to Java and Bali were part of a series of lecture tours he undertook to share with other Asian countries his ideal of a unified Eastern civilization. Before beginning his journey, Rabindranath had stated that he was going on a pilgrimage to India beyond its modern political boundaries.

As he landed at Jakarta's Tanjung Priok harbour in August 1927, Tagore was enchanted. He spoke in praise of the 'golden threads of kinship that existed between Indonesia and India.' His travels around the country drew enthusiastic crowds. In Java one of his closest allies was Ki Hajar Dewantoro, founder of the Taman Siswa schools and the country's first minister of education. Dewantoro was inspired by Rabindranath's ideas, and also by his school at Santiniketan and his university Visva-Bharati. Dewantoro, the painter Affandi and Dr Ida Bagus Mantra of Bali visited Rabindranath's university of universal learning In Java, Rabindranath saw the remains of ancient Indian civilization in locations such as Borobudur, a Mahayana Buddhist temple complex dating back to the 9th century. He described these experiences in *Java Jatrir Patra*.

13 ✒ The Final Journey

From 1937, Rabindranath's health worsened. He lost consciousness on several occasions. His intellect remained undimmed despite illness. He continued to write poems and stories which were published as *Se* (1937), *Tin Sangi* (1940), and *Galpasalpa* (1941). On August 7, 1941, he passed away after a prolonged illness at Thakurbari, the house in Jorasanko where he had been born. He was eighty years old. Shocked and sorrowful crowds swarmed the streets of Calcutta as his body was carried away for the funeral. The 22nd of *Shravan* continues to be observed as Rabindranath's death anniversary.

Rabindranath's work and ideas continue to inspire writers, intellectuals and even ordinary people all over the world. Great modern leaders like Nelson Mandela of South Africa and Aung San Suu Kyi of Myanmar have acknowledged him as an inspiration. Rabindranath is the only person in history to have composed the national anthems of two countries; India (*Jana Gana Mana*) and Bangladesh (*Amar Sonar Bangla*).

Rabindranath was an international figure. He evolved, in the words of former Indian President Pratibha Patil, into 'a strong proponent of promoting international peace and understanding . . . the untiring pacifist who wrote to foster unity, harmony and peace.'

With a renewed interest in humanism in today's world, people everywhere are rediscovering the vision and brilliance of Rabindranath.

TRIVIA
TREASURY

Turn the pages to discover more fascinating facts and tantalizing tidbits of history about this legendary life and his world.

WHAT HAPPENED AND WHEN

- **1861**: Rabindranath is born in Thakurbari, Jorasanko, Calcutta to Sarada Devi and Maharshi Debendranath Tagore.
- **1869**: Mahatma Gandhi is born in Porbander, Gujarat.
- **1873**: Rabindranath's *upanayan* or sacred thread ceremony is performed. His father, the Maharshi, takes him on his first long journey to the Himalayas. On the way, the young Rabi visits Santiniketan for the first time.
- **1875**: Rabindranath's mother Sarada Devi passes away.
- **1876**: Queen Victoria becomes Empress of India.
- **1877**: Rabindranath's first poems are published under a pen name, Bhanu Singh Thakur.
- **1878**: Rabindranath stays with his brother Satyendranath in Ahmedabad. He sets sail for his first trip to England later in the same year.
- **1879**: Rabindranath takes admission in University College, Cambridge.
- **1883**: Rabindranath marries Mrinalini Devi.
- **1884**: *Bhagnahriday*, a collection of poems largely composed during Rabindranath's stay in England, is

published. Kadambari Devi (Notun Bouthan) dies tragically at the age of twenty-five.

- **1885**: Burma becomes a province of India. The Indian National Congress is formed.
- **1886**: Publication of *Kari o Komal*.
- **1890**: Publication of *Manashi*.
- **1891**: Rabindranath takes charge of the family estates in Shelidah. Writes 'Postmaster'.
- **1894**: *Shonar Tari* is published.
- **1900**: *Galpaguccha*, Rabindranath's first collection of short stories, is published.
- **1901**: Rabindranath's school is inaugurated in Santiniketan on 23 December.
- **1905**: Lord Curzon, the British Viceroy, partitions Bengal into Hindu and Muslim sections. Bengal is reunited in 1911. Rabindranath becomes involved in the Swadeshi Movement.
- **1906**: Gandhiji coins the word satyagraha in South Africa. All India Muslim League is formed.
- **1907**: Rabindranath's novel *Gora* first appears serialized in *Pravasi* magazine.
- **1910**: Rabindranath arranges the marriage of his son Rathindranath to a young widow, Pratima Devi. Rabindranath writes the poems in *Gitanjali* in Bengali.
- **1911**: India's capital shifted from Calcutta to Delhi. Rabindranath writes *Jana Gana Mana*, which later becomes India's national anthem. Writes the play *Dak Ghar*. *Jibansmriti* (My Reminiscences) serialized in *Pravasi* magazine.

- **1912**: *Gitanjali* published in English.
- **1913**: Rabindranath awarded the Nobel Prize for Literature.
- **1915**: King George confers the knighthood on Rabindranath.
- **1917**: Gandhiji's satyagraha campaign begins at Champaran, Bihar.
- **1919**: The Jalianwala Bagh Massacre in Amritsar. Rabindranath surrenders knighthood in protest.
- **1921**: Rabindranath sets up Visva–Bharati University in Santiniketan.
- **1929**: Rabindranath begins painting.
- **1930**: Gandhiji's Dandi March; launching the Civil Disobedience Movement.
- **1940**: Jinnah demands a separate new country called Pakistan for Muslims.
- **1941**: Rabindranath passes away in Thakurbari, the house where he had been born.

MEANWHILE, ELSEWHERE IN THE WORLD

- **1861**: Abraham Lincoln is elected the sixteenth president of the US. American Civil War begins. The abolition of slavery is a core issue. In Russia, the serfs are given freedom.

- **1865**: Abraham Lincoln is assassinated. American Civil War ends.
- **1876**: Alexander Graham Bell of the USA invents the telephone.
- **1879**: Thomas Edison of the USA invents the electric light bulb.
- **1886**: The first car is invented by Karl Benz in Germany.
- **1899–1902** The Boer Wars are fought in South Africa.
- **1900**: Boxer Rebellion in China.
- **1901**: British colonies in Australia unite to form the Commonwealth of Australia.
- **1903**: The first plane successfully flown by the Wright Brothers of the USA.
- **1904–1905** War between Russia and Japan.
- **1906**: A terrible earthquake wreaks havoc in San Francisco, USA.
- **1910**: Japan overruns Korea.
  Apartheid (political and legal discrimination against people based on their race and colour of skin) introduced in South Africa.
- **1911**: Amundsen becomes the first man to reach the South Pole.
- **1912**: The Titanic sinks. Thousands die.
- **1914**: World War I begins on 28 July 1914. The War ends on 11 November 1918.
- **1914**: The Panama Canal opens, drastically reducing the distance and time ships need to travel from the Atlantic Ocean to reach the Pacific Ocean.

- **1916**: The Easter Rising takes place in Ireland against British rule.
- **1917**: The Bolshevik Revolution takes place in Russia, as people rise against Tsar Nicholas II. Lenin and Trotsky take over as rulers, and Communists come into power in Russia.
- **1919**: Treaty of Versailles is signed.
- **1921**: Southern Ireland gains independence from British rule.
- **1922**: Mussolini takes control of Italy. The Soviet Union is formed.
- **1924**: The death of Lenin.
- **1927**: Charles Lindberg is the first man to fly across the Atlantic.
- **1928**: Alexander Fleming discovers penicillin, the first antibiotic which can cure many deadly diseases. Stalin gains full control over Russia.
- **1929**: The stock markets crash on Wall Street, New York, beginning The Great Depression, which grips economies around the world.
- **1933**: Adolf Hitler becomes ruler of Germany. Franklin Roosevelt becomes President of the USA.
- **1934**: Mao Zedong leads the Long March in China.
- **1939**: World War II begins in 1939, and ends in 1945 with the surrender of Germany and Japan.

  The German army continues its aggressive thrust across Europe, and invades Poland. Britain and France declare war on Germany. Russia attacks Finland.

- **1941**: Germany overruns Yugoslavia and Greece, and invades Russia.
  Japan attacks Pearl Harbour (USA).
  USA joins World War II on the side of the Allied Powers (Britain, France etc).

RENAISSANCE IN BENGAL

Rabindranath was the Renaissance Man of India; a man who shone in every artistic and intellectual field. Let's take a look at the historical and cultural background against which his genius blossomed.

The Bengal Renaissance of the 19th century was a result of several centuries of sweeping cultural and social reforms. As Bengalis gained exposure to Western education and ideas, they challenged deeply-ingrained orthodox practices such as denying education to women, a rigid caste system, sati and dowry, all of which were hindering the progress of the community. Raja Ram Mohan Roy (1774–1833) was at the vanguard of this movement. He spearheaded the challenging of age-old orthodox social evils such as the burning of widows, and paved the way for religious and social reforms.

Henry Louis Vivian Derozio (1809–1831) along with David Hare (1775–1841) was responsible for spreading European learning and science among the people of Bengal. Pandit Iswar Chandra Vidyasagar (1820–1891) championed widow remarriage. Scholar and social reformer Vidyasagar together with Drinkwater Bethune founded the Bethune School, where girls could gain formal education for the first time. Other path-breaking intellectuals of this period were Maharshi Debendranath Tagore, Akshay Kumar Datta, Michael Madhusudan Dutt, Bankim Chandra Chattopadhyay and Swami Vivekananda. Inspired by these powerful thinkers and social leaders, people began to take pride in the newly evolving concept of India as a nation. They began to challenge India's subjugation to foreign rule.

During the Bengal Renaissance, many newspapers and magazines appeared. People organized themselves into progressive societies and organizations. Religious and social reform movements took root and flourished. In this way, people expressed and spread new ideas and created forums for debates on social issues. All these led to social change and advancement.

One of the earliest social movements of this time was the Young Bengal Movement, comprising mainly of educated Bengali youth who were disciples of the poet and thinker Derozio. They aimed to put established Hindu ideas and practices to the test of reason. They boldly advocated rationalism, and appreciated and assimilated invigorating new ideas from the West.

The socio-religious reformist movement of the Brahmo Samaj also gained momentum at this time. The Brahmos traced their intellectual roots to the

Upanishads. They rejected prevailing social evils such as polygamy and sati, and believed in a single supreme divine power. Many Brahmos also took the lead in the emerging freedom movement. Although Hindu society accepted most of these ideas and social reforms, the Brahmo Samaj remained by and large an elitist movement.

In the decades after the Indian Rebellion of 1857, Bengali literature saw a brilliant burst of creativity. Writers like Bankim Chandra Chattopadhyay expressed and popularized the new ideas and ideals through their literary art.

Shri Ramakrishna Paramhansa, a great saint of Bengal, saw the basic underlying spiritual truths common to all religions and sects. Through his teachings, he tried to nurture tolerance and acceptance of other religions. Shri Ramakrishna's disciple Swami Vivekananda urged Indians to break free from the chains of colonial rule, and visualized a free, progressive and prosperous India. In his view, to love humanity and all living beings was to truly serve God. He made a brilliant presentation on Hinduism at the Parliament of the World's Religions in Chicago in 1893, and continued to disseminate in the West the greatness of Indian philosophy and ideals during a lecture tour in America.

Critics of the Bengal Renaissance hold that it was restricted to urban upper-class Bengalis with exposure to Western education. Its effects and benefits did not percolate to the underprivileged people of the cities, the large Muslim population of Bengal, and the people who lived in the rural heartland. There was indeed a predominance of Hindu reformers and intellectuals. However, there were also some noteworthy Muslim intellectual leaders. Delawar Hosaen (1840–1913) was a rationalist thinker on Muslim socio-economic problems. Mir Mosharraf Hossain (1847–1912) was a remarkable novelist, playwright and social critic. Rokeya Sakhawat Hossain (1880–1932) the prominent Muslim woman writer and educationist, championed the cause of emancipating Muslim women.

The Tagore family, which had imbibed both Indian and Western influences, rose to prominence during the Bengal Renaissance. As Pirali Brahmins, they were considered a lower class by the orthodox Brahmins, who kept a social distance from them. So they were less inhibited by the fear of social ostracism, and felt free to absorb progressive Western ideas and education. Since many of the Tagores belonged to the Brahmo Samaj, they were a part of Hindu society in all respects except that they did not worship idols. This combination of influences gave the Tagores a firm grounding in Hindu ideas and ideals, but they could also boldly question established orthodox practices.

The Tagore family played a major role in the Bengal Renaissance. They were leaders in politics and commerce as well as in the fields of arts, music and literature. They also took an active part in patriotic movements of their time, such as the Hindu Mela, the Congress and the National Conference, the Rakhi Festival of 1905, and the anti-partition movement.

RABINDRANATH TAGORE'S 150TH BIRTH ANNIVERSARY CELEBRATIONS IN INDIA AND WORLDWIDE 2011–2012

- Rabindranath's 150th birth anniversary celebrations set off a flurry of cultural activities and commemorative functions all over India. Awards were instituted, commemorative stamps were issued, and a substantial government grant was made to revitalize Visva-Bharati, among many other projects.

- Leaders of India and Bangladesh joined hands to celebrate the 150th birth anniversary of Rabindranath Tagore on 6 May 2011. Rabindranath belonged to all of Bengal, and indeed to all of humanity. Such joint international celebrations were in keeping with his spirit of universal human brotherhood.

- Among other joint projects, India and Bangladesh are also working on introducing a travel circuit covering his birthplace, Jorasanko Thakurbari, and Santiniketan in West Bengal, and places he frequented in Bangladesh, such as Shelaidah, Kushtia, Shahzadpur and Patesar.

- In Sri Lanka on the 150th birth anniversary of Rabindranath Tagore, his bust was unveiled at the University of Colombo. Rabindranath's three visits to the island nation between 1922, 1928 and 1934 had created an abiding influence on Sri Lankan art and culture. He helped inspire the country's cultural rebirth. Prominent Sri Lankan intellectuals and artists such as Ananda Samarakoon (composer of the Sri Lankan national anthem), Chitrasena and Sunil Shantha attended Visva-Bharati University and were influenced by Rabindranath. Rabindranath too, was impressed by the Kandyan dance and mask dance of the country. He integrated some aspects of those dances in his own choreographic productions.

- Rabindranath continues to be remembered in the countries he visited.
- Spain celebrated his anniversary in 2011 with a compendium, *Redescubriendo a Tagore* (Rethinking Tagore).
- Berlin has installed many busts in bronze to commemorate Rabindranath's affinity with the Bauhaus artists he visited in Weimar in 1921. Rabindranath, along with his nephew the great artist Abanindranath, had organized the first ever large-scale exhibition of Bauhaus masters outside Europe. They exhibited works by artists like Wassily Kandinsky and Paul Klee, among others, in Kolkata in 1923.
- Busts and statues of the poet stand in his honour in places as far as Astana, Havana, Valladolid, Vancouver, Fiji, Dublin, Ankara, Toronto, Tashkent, Budapest, Bucharest, Berlin, Paris, New York, Mexico and Mauritius. A towering statue sculpted by Ram Sutar

graces a park in Moscow next to Rechnoy Vokzal metro station.

- As a great Indian and an intellectual who belonged to the entire world, Rabindranath continues to be honoured everywhere.

BOOKS TO READ

Here are some books you can read if you want to know more about Rabindranath and his works. Continue to browse through libraries and the Internet for more interesting stuff.

1. *The Land of Cards: Stories, Poems and Plays for Children* by Rabindranath Tagore (Penguin Books India, 2010)
2. *Rabindranath Tagore Omnibus* (Rupa & Co, 2003)
3. *Puffin Classics: Boyhood Days by Rabindranath Tagore*, (eds.) Radha Chakravarty, Amartya Sen (Penguin Books India, 2007)
4. *Selected Short Stories* by Rabindranath Tagore (Oxford University Press, 2001)
5. *My Life in My Words* by Rabindranath Tagore, (ed.) Uma Dasgupta (Penguin Books India, 2010)
6. *Rabindranath Tagore; A Biography*, (ed.) Uma Dasgupta (Oxford University Press, 2004)
7. *Rabindranath Tagore* Kalyanaksha Banerjee (Amar Chitra Katha, 1977)

Other Books in the Series

Chanakya: The Master of Statecraft
By Deepa Agarwal

'I, Chanakya, vow not to bind my hair until I have unseated you from the throne of Magadha.'

When learned Brahmin Vishnugupta is humiliated by arrogant king Dhana Nanda in a public gathering, he swears revenge. Anger is his weakness, but strategy, his strength. This formerly unknown Brahmin goes on to become the most well-known kingmaker in Indian history, Chanakya. Using a combination of cunning, ruthlessness and luck, Chanakya fulfils his vow and propels a boy of unknown origins, Chandragupta Maurya, to the throne of the most powerful kingdom of that time, an empire even Alexander the Great hesitated to confront.

This fascinating account shows how Chanakya went from being a penniless fugitive with the rebel prince of Pataliputra to the prime minister of Magadha, and finally the author of the groundbreaking *Arthashastra*. With fun snippets and lesser-known facts about Chanakya and the Mauryan age, this book promises to be an exciting and gripping adventure story.

Other Books in the Series

Rani Lakshmibai: The Valiant Queen of Jhansi
By *Deepa Agarwal*

The elephant obediently sank on its knees, responding to its mahout's commands. Three men mounted it. A little girl came running up. 'Wait, I want to ride it too! I want to ride it too!' she clamoured. The men ignored her pointedly. Her father Moropant pulled her away. 'It's not in your destiny to ride elephants,' he said.

The girl's large eyes flashed. 'It's my destiny to ride ten. Wait and see, Baba!'

A little girl Manikarnika, with an uncanny sense of her own destiny, grew up to be none other than the brave queen of Jhansi, Rani Lakshmibai. Trained in horse riding and the martial arts from an early age, Manu was married to Gangadhar Rao, the Maharaja of Jhansi, when she was thirteen. Soon after her husband's death, the reins of the kingdom passed on to her, and she took up this responsibility undeterred and fearless. When Jhansi faced the danger of annexation, she fought against the British with unflinching courage, losing her life in the course of the battle. She has since become one of the most inspiring heroes of the freedom struggle and a much-admired role model.

Deepa Agarwal chronicles the life and times of this legendary character in a gripping narrative, drawing a colourful portrait of bravery. This riveting account also includes nuggets of information about the eventful year 1857, making for a fascinating read.

Other Books in the Series

Jawaharlal Nehru: The Jewel of India
By Aditi De

At midnight on 14 August 1947, Jawaharlal Nehru rose to speak to independent India as its first Prime Minister. He was dressed in a pale cream *achkan*, a white khadi cap on his head. Though his eyes had shadows beneath them, they grew brighter as Jawaharlal began to speak . . .

Pandit Nehru's words that night have remained etched in the nation's memory ever since. Born to a privileged family in Allahabad, Jawaharlal went on to become a leading figure of the Indian independence movement. During the struggle he spent over ten years in prison, watched others in his family jailed time and again, and led numerous protest marches and agitations. Working alongside Mahatma Gandhi, he helped India keep its tryst with destiny and become a free nation.

Aditi De recounts the story of Jawaharlal Nehru's extraordinary life in this sparkling biography for young readers. Filled with charming anecdotes, it recounts episodes from Nehru's childhood, and how he was drawn to the growing struggle for Indian independence. She sketches his role as the first Indian Prime Minister, and how he shaped the newly-formed democratic republic. Packed with little-known nuggets of information, and trivia about the times, this book in the *Puffin Lives* series brings alive the thoughts and actions of one of modern India's most important personalities.

Other Books in the Series

Mahatma Gandhi: The Father of the Nation
By Subhadra Sen Gupta

On his passport he was Mohandas Karamchand Gandhi. The poet Rabindranath Tagore gave him the title 'Mahatma' the great soul but he was rather uncomfortable with that. Nelson Mandela calls him a 'sacred warrior', others describe him as the 'the saint of the spinning wheel' and we now declare him as our 'Father of the Nation'.

A courageous freedom fighter, a shrewd politician, a passionate social reformer and a staunch nationalist, Mahatma Gandhi was all this and much more. He was the most unusual leader this country has seen, and one of the most influential personalities whose name is synonymous with India's independence. He was the one who touched the lives of millions, whose ideals of satyagraha and ahimsa inspired great leaders of the world, and who could make the entire country come to a halt by going on a fast. This is the fascinating story of Gandhiji's life, of the ideals and principles that shaped him, and the eccentric fads and fancies that set him apart.

Through a vivid narrative, author Subhadra Sen Gupta recreates the life and legacy of this phenomenal leader to portray the man beneath the simple handspun clothes, who ate saltless vegetables and bitter neem chutney; who greeted kings and paupers alike; who walked 240 miles at the age of sixty to break the Salt Law; and whose entire life was dedicated to truth and to peace. Even today as we read inspirational accounts of Gandhiji's life and talk of *gandhigiri,* we know that his ideals are alive and relevant to today's generation.